LEWIS & CLARK'S
Montana Trail

TEXT AND PHOTOS BY RICK AND SUSIE GRAETZ
AERIAL PHOTOGRAPHY BY LARRY MAYER
FOREWORD BY STEPHEN E. AMBROSE

The Montana Series

NUMBER 8 EIGHT

"The hills and river Clifts which we passed today exhibit a most romantic appearance....With the help of a little immagination... are made to represent eligant ranges of lofty freestone buildings... it seemed as if those seens of visionary inchantmnet would never have and end." —MERIWETHER LEWIS

PHOTOGRAPHY CONTRIBUTIONS BY:

Erwin and Peggy Bauer ▪ Douglass Dye ▪ Chuck Haney ▪ John Lambing ▪ Donnie Sexton/Travel Montana

We would like to acknowledge the many folks who aided us with this project. Their time, intelligence, advice, and kindness will not be forgotten.

For reading chapters, correcting facts or guiding us along the route, we owe an enormous debt of gratitude to: Stephen Ambrose, Mareta Brusett, Chuck Cook, Buck Damone, Bob Doerk, Troy Helmick, Myrtle Hubley, Sherman Hubley, Jack Lepley, Nancy Maxson, Roscoe Montgomery, Joseph Mussulman, Don Peterson, Linda Twitchell, Mike Varone and Jane Weber.

To those landowners who allowed us access to sites related to the Expedition...Greg Gannon, Don Lundy, Harry Mitchell and Neil Snyder, the privilege was much appreciated.

And a special thanks to Dave Mari and his staff at the BLM Lewistown Field Office.

The Journals of the Lewis and Clark Expedition, edited by Gary Moulton, make fascinating reading. The amount of research that went into this project, with the valuable footnotes a layman could use, make them a worthwhile investment. They are available wherever books are sold or from the publisher, the University of Nebraska Press. 1-800-526-2617 (nebraskapress.UNL@edu). Volumes 4, 5 and 8 are pertinent to Montana.

©2001 Northern Rockies Publishing
Rick and Susie Graetz
P.O. Box 1707, Helena, Montana 59624
norockpub@aol.com

Book design by GingerBee, Helena, Montana

All color and prepress work done in Montana, U.S.A.
Printed in Korea
Softcover: ISBN 1-891152-13-0
Hardcover: ISBN 1-891152-14-9

E.W. Paxson *Lewis and Clark At Three Forks* mural at Montana State Capitol, oil on canvas, 1912.

COURTESY OF THE MONTANA HISTORICAL SOCIETY

Front Cover:
The White Cliffs at Eagle Creek in the Upper Missouri River Breaks National Monument — Lewis and Clark camped here May 31, 1805.

RICK AND SUSIE GRAETZ

FOREWORD
BY STEPHEN E. AMBROSE

Lewis and Clark spent more time in Montana than in any other state. And they saw more in Montana than anywhere else. They noted and recorded the sites — grasslands, plains, river valleys and gorges and canyons, immense mountains, an astonishing number of new plants and animals to describe, the Great Falls, Three Forks, Lemhi Pass. It was therefore appropriate that when Meriwether Lewis wrote his great line, *"As we passed on it seemed as if those seens of visionary inchantment would never have and end,"* he was in Montana.

Threading through the whole of Montana is the Missouri River and its principal tributaries, including the Marias River, the Judith River, Arrow River (named *"Slaughter River"* by the captains), the Milk River, the Sun River (called *"Medicine River"* by the Indians, and others). It forms up at Three Forks, in southwestern Montana, at the junction of the Madison, Gallatin, and Jefferson rivers (all named by the captains). The biggest of the Missouri's tributaries is the Yellowstone River, rising in today's Yellowstone National Park and gathering in its tributaries, flowing first north, then east to its junction with the Missouri, near today's Montana-North Dakota state line. Combined, these rivers tie and hold the state of Montana together in the same way the two strong yet distinct personalities, intelligence and leadership qualities of Lewis and Clark formed, directed and held the Corps of Discovery together.

Montana also presented the captains with some of their most challenging predicaments (which way? the *"north fork"* — Marias or the *"south fork"* — Missouri), and obstacles (portaging the Great Falls, weather extremes, an abundance of rattlesnakes, mosquitoes and prickly pear cactus to name only a few), as well as an opportunity to show their uncanny ability to determine the best solution and to stick by their convictions. It was in Montana where the men of the Corps exhibited their unwavering confidence in and cheerful willingness to follow the two commanders.

In the Missouri River Breaks National Monument, designated by President Clinton in 2001, there is a section where an extensive labyrinth of coulees and canyons extend outward from the river much further than anywhere else in the Monument. Lewis called it *"truly a desert barren country,"* while Clark described the sector as *"the Deserts of America."* On May 26, 1805, at this eastern end of the Breaks, Lewis climbed the surrounding bluffs, a *"fortiegueing"* task, but he thought himself *"well repaid for any labour"* when he reached the highest spot in the neighborhood, because *"from this point I beheld the Rocky Mountains for the first time…When I viewed these mountains I felt a secret pleasure in finding myself so near the head of the heretofore conceived boundless Missouri."*

Modern Montana scholars insist that what Lewis was looking at on May 26 was the Bears Paw Mountains, not the Rockies proper. The Bears Paw are an outreach of the Rockies, but for my part I'm not about to correct Meriwether Lewis on a geographical fact. If he says he saw the Rockies, as far as I'm concerned, he did.

And it was yet in Montana, later, in August, 1805, when climbing to Lemhi Pass, Lewis came to a spring bubbling up from a spot almost at the Continental Divide (and today's Montana-Idaho state line). He called it *"the most distant fountain of the waters of the mighty Missouri in search of*

which we have spent so many toilsome days and wristless night," and noted that one of his soldiers *"had exultingly stood with a foot on each side of this little rivulet and thanked his god that he had lived to bestride the mighty & heretofore deemed endless Missouri."*

At Camp Fortunate on August 17, 1805, Lewis and Clark successfully negotiated with the Shoshone Indians (Sacajawea's people), for the horses they needed to cross the rugged and unpredictable Rocky Mountains. Leaving their canoes behind, the Corps of Discovery began the overland portion of the journey out of Montana and on to the Pacific.

No one has ever captured the essence of Lewis and Clark in Montana as well as Rick and Susie Graetz. They have keen eyes, equally discriminating and imaginative, in picking out photographic sites, or judging the light and composition, or deciding on what story to tell, or choosing the captains' words in the Journals to quote. Their descriptions of the campsites along the way are exact and invite the modern traveler to visit those places. In this book, they guide you to the right spots, and much is richer with their photographs of the sites today.

STEPHEN E. AMBROSE is the author of the highly acclaimed account of the Lewis and Clark Expedition, *Undaunted Courage* and numerous other best selling historical books. He spends his summers in Montana and the cold months in Mississippi.

From the Eye of the Needle looking downriver, a landscape Lewis described as *"seens of visionary inchantment."*
RICK AND SUSIE GRAETZ

THE LEWIS AND CLARK INTERPRETIVE CENTER

Discovering the *"great falls"* of the Missouri was one of the highlights of the Corps of Discovery's Montana journey...portaging the five of them was probably the most difficult task. The Lewis & Clark National Historic Trail Interpretive Center, a *"living, breathing history book,"* as the Great Falls Tribune describes it, is located on the banks of the Missouri in the area of the falls on the northern edge of Great Falls, Montana.

To spend a day here is to step back into the Expedition. The place can be likened to a *"nerve center"* of the Corps of Discovery's time in Montana. Not only can you can trace the route of the explorers up the Missouri from St. Louis to its headwaters in Montana, then across the Northern Rocky Mountains to the Pacific Ocean and return, but you can also get a great appreciation for the difficulty and diversity of the journey.

Operated by the U.S. Forest Service, the central theme of this 25,000 square foot treasure house is Lewis and Clark's life amongst the Plains Indians. While you learn the intricacies of the Expedition, you'll also leave with some understanding of the different Indian Nations they encountered and relied heavily on for assistance. In keeping with this theme, the Interpretive Center features a 28-minute, PBS documentary film produced by award winning director Ken Burns.

How the Expedition packed their "baggage," and why they made the caches, what plants and animals they saw, how did the Indians live and what was their reaction to Lewis and Clark, what was the iron boat like? These are just a few of the many questions answered through the panels and interactive displays in the exhibit hall.

Of special interest is a large map compiled from the original drawings of William Clark showing the area they covered. Was there a life for Expedition members when their historical journey ended? The Center has the answer for the explorers as well as the fate of the Indian tribes.

Opportunities for hands-on demonstrations, short programs, presentations and events are numerous; one day may not be enough for a visit. The research library itself demands time. The national archives of the Lewis and Clark Trail Heritage Foundation is located in the Center. This public library has more than 1,000 books and documents on hand, many of them rare or one-of-a-kind. As a result, the center attracts many well known Lewis and Clark scholars.

For more information call 406-727-8733 or visit www.fs.fed.us/r1/lewisclark/lcic.htm

A two-story, life-size portrayal of the portage of the *"great falls,"* greets visitors at the Lewis and Clark Interpretive Center.
RICK AND SUSIE GRAETZ

6

Camp
Disappointment

Marias River

Teton River

Mouth

Sun River

Great
Falls

Fort
Benton

Great Falls o
the Missouri

Clark Fork

Lewis and
Clark Pass

Dearborn

Lewis and Clark
Interpretive Cente

River

Blackfoot River

Gates
of the Mountains

Judit

Missoula

Lolo Pass

Travelers'
Rest

Clark Fork River

Helena

Bitterroot R.

Ross'
Hole

Big Hole River

Three Forks of
the Missouri

Jefferson River

Bozeman

Rive

Lost Trail
Pass

Livingst

Madison River

Gallatin River

Yellowstone

Lemhi
Pass

Dillon

Beaverhead R.

Camp
Fortunate

Shoshone
Villages

N

miles

0   40

Map © 9/01
Great Divide GeoGraphics
Helena, Montana
emadej@qwest.net

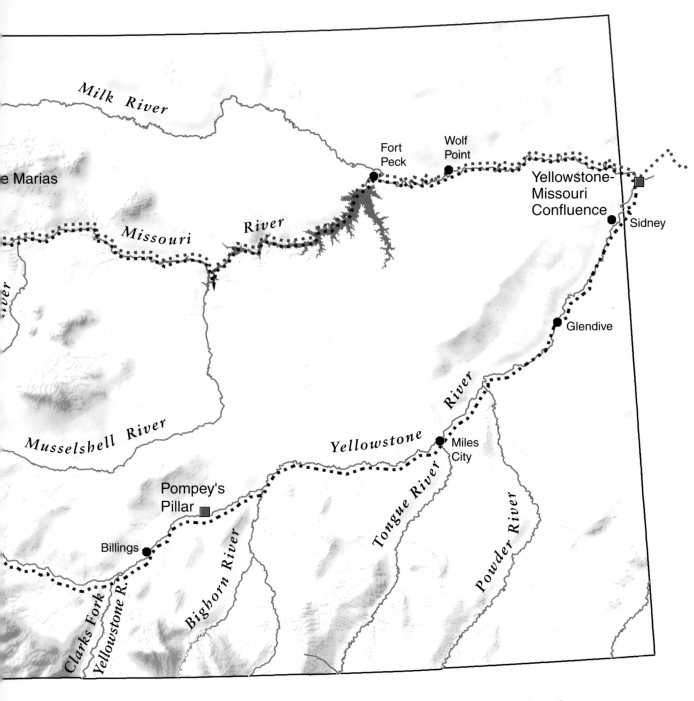

Milk River

Fort Peck

Wolf Point

e Marias

Missouri River

Yellowstone-
Missouri
Confluence

Sidney

Glendive

Musselshell River

Yellowstone River

Miles
City

Pompey's
Pillar

River

Tongue River

Powder River

Billings

Clarks Fork

Bigborn River

Yellowstone R.

Legend

Westbound — 1805

Eastbound — 1806

Sites of Interest

GETTING STARTED

The journey of Lewis and Clark and their Corps of Discovery was one of the most powerful events in our nation's history. To quote Roy Appleman in his publication written for a National Park Service, *"...they carried the destiny as well as the flag of our young Nation westward, from the Mississippi across thousands of miles of mostly unknown land...up the Missouri, over the Rocky Mountains and on to the Pacific. This epic feat not only sparked national pride, but also fired the imagination of the American people and made them feel for the first time the full sweep of the continent on which they lived."*

Without Thomas Jefferson's foresight and persistence, Lewis and Clark's voyage into history would never have taken place. Well before ascending to the presidency of the United States, this learned man from Monticello, Virginia had a strong interest in the West. His election victory provided him with the power and opportunity to pursue that curiosity.

In his 1801 inaugural speech, Jefferson told the nation that it was imperative to see beyond our present limits and *"look forward to distant times."* He warned that our growing population and interests would necessitate the new nation to cover the entire continent.

The idea to explore the Missouri River to its source and beyond was President Jefferson's. In 1802 he sent emissaries to France to attempt the purchase of New Orleans. Napoleon instead offered to sell all of the Louisiana Territory, and the U.S. accepted. Negotiations however were still needed, Congress had to be involved and the sale would take time. Even without being certain of an actual purchase, on January 18, 1803, in a secret message to Congress, Jefferson asked for an appropriation of $2,500 to cover the cost of the exploration. In order to push his agenda through, he somewhat disguised the true purpose of the mission by putting the request in terms of commerce.

Once the expedition was completed, the actual costs would total $38,722.25. In the words of Bob Doerk, former president of the Lewis & Clark Heritage Trail Foundation (www.lewisandclark.org), it would be *"one of the first examples of a U.S. government cost overrun."*

The expedition needed a strong leader and Jefferson readily found one in his personal secretary Meriwether Lewis. In him the president saw traits that would greatly add to the success of the mission. Not having been highly educated, in order to prepare for the trip, Lewis was tutored in the many sciences. In June of 1803, Lewis wrote to the man, who before leaving the army, had been his commanding officer in the 1790s. He offered William Clark an equal partnership in leading the Expedition.

Lewis, a captain, asked that Clark be commissioned the same. The War Department however turned down the request and instead bestowed the rank of lieutenant on Clark. Lewis remaining true to his promise, considered him his equal and referred to him as captain. The members of the Expedition never knew the difference, they saw the two men as sharing the command.

These two captains with their different skills and personalities complemented each other. Clark was a geographer-cartographer and Lewis a naturalist; and Clark was outgoing, while Lewis had more of a reserved demeanor.

In the Missouri River Canyon and the Gates of the Mountains area — Lewis passed through here on July 19, 1805.
RICK AND SUSIE GRAETZ

In the spring of 1803, the treaty to purchase the Louisiana Territory was signed and on July 4, 1803, the news from Europe arrived announcing, *"the United States have obtained full right to and sovereignty over New Orleans, and the whole of Louisiana."* Exploration of this territory would now include diplomatic duties.

Transfer of ownership of Louisiana Territory involved politics and an arrogant and misguided attitude that the original inhabitants of the land had no right to it. The real fact was the land Lewis and Clark were to enter had been lived on by countless generations of Indians. They would have to tell these tribes that their homeland was now owned by a government they had never seen or knew anything about.

Most of the Indians extended the hand of friendship to the Expedition as well as food, horses and information. Too often those who followed betrayed this hospitable welcome. Within 80 years of the Journey, most tribes were restricted to reservations.

The date of the inauguration of the Expedition is left open to opinion. The official Bicentennial Celebration commences on January 18, 2003, two hundred years after Jefferson asked for the appropriation. Some scholars feel it began when Clark accepted Lewis's invitation, others believe it to be when Lewis left Pittsburgh on August 31, 1803, to move down the Ohio River with his completed keelboat. Then there is the thought that the date is October 15th when Lewis and Clark met and shook hands, sealing their agreement.

With their Corps of Discovery, the two captains left Camp Dubois near St. Louis, Missouri on May 14, 1804, to embark on one of history's most storied expeditions. Specifically, Jefferson's instructions were…*"the object of your mission is to explore the Missouri River & such principle stream of it, as, by its course and communication with the waters of the Pacific Ocean may offer the most direct & practical water communication across this continent for the purposes of commerce."*

Prior to their trip, the West was virgin territory passed through by only a few white explorers; a mysterious place that stirred the imagination. Lewis and Clark received much of their information on what lay ahead in Montana from the Minnetarees or Hidatsa Indians, while spending the winter of 1803–1804 at Fort Mandan near present-day Bismarck, North Dakota.

It took nearly a year after leaving St. Louis for the party to reach the confluence of the Missouri and Yellowstone rivers, in the northwest corner of North Dakota. On April 27, 1805, after having spent a short time at the meeting of these great rivers, the Corps entered what eventually would become Montana Territory.

The explorers spent four months following the Missouri through eastern and central Montana, past the future sites of Great Falls and Helena to what is now Three Forks and the commencement of the Missouri's surge. They then routed up the Jefferson River to the Beaverhead to its origins at the joining of Red Rock and Horse Prairie creeks, today the site of Clark Canyon Reservoir. From there, they traversed west through the Horse Prairie Creek Valley to Lemhi Pass, arriving on the Continental Divide and the Idaho border on August 12, 1805.

Their path then proceeded down the west side of the Divide to Idaho's Lemhi River Valley, trailed north to the Salmon River and then back into Montana again via the Lost Trail Pass area. Moving up the Bitterroot Valley to a place they called Travelers' Rest near present day Lolo, the Corps turned west again crossing Lolo Pass into Idaho on September 13, 1805, and eventually found

▸▸ The Missouri River above Cascade.
RICK AND SUSIE GRAETZ

their way to the Pacific Ocean.

On June 29, 1806 on their return journey from the coast, they once more ventured through Lolo Pass and back to Travelers' Rest. Here the leaders split, Lewis proceeded through present-day Missoula up the Blackfoot River and across today's Lewis and Clark's Pass, northeast of Lincoln. Attaining the Continental Divide at this point, Lewis and his men trekked to the Sun River and eventually were reunited with the Missouri. Lewis made an exploratory trip up the Marias River north towards today's Cut Bank and Browning region and then came back to the Missouri and headed downstream.

Clark, upon leaving Travelers' Rest, retraced part of their previous route up the Bitterroot River and then entered the Big Hole Valley on his way to a cache they had left near Horse Prairie Creek at Camp Fortunate. He then navigated the Beaverhead and Jefferson rivers to Three Forks, turned east through the Gallatin Valley and on to the Yellowstone River, following it to the Missouri where he rejoined Lewis. The Expedition continued to St. Louis, reaching the terminus of their adventure on September 23, 1806.

It would be difficult to identify another adventure on American soil as great as this one. In reading what these 30 men, one woman, an infant and a Newfoundland dog experienced is almost unbelievable...the incredible physical toil, often hindered by nature's surprises from the sky, as well as her creatures, both large and small, seemed to be more than any humans could handle. Success was their reward.

Sunset over the
mountains of Idaho
from Lemhi Pass.
RICK AND SUSIE GRAETZ

The bitterroot flower
was first identified by
Lewis in Montana
in 1805.
RICK AND SUSIE GRAETZ

Below the Iron City
Islands in an area
Clark referred to as
"*the Deserts of
America.*"
RICK AND SUSIE GRAETZ

THE CORPS OF DISCOVERY IN MONTANA

The time spent in Montana recording this momentous exploit was significant; it provided Lewis and Clark with some of their most memorable experiences, as well as periods of extreme hardship. Counting their odyssey to the Pacific Coast and the return passage to St. Louis, the explorers stayed nearly six months in Montana.

Before setting out to follow their trail through Big Sky Country, prepare yourself by studying some of the many resources available. First, read Stephen Ambrose's *Undaunted Courage*. This masterpiece of writing not only depicts the entire epic, but also offers insight into the two captains' thinking and observations and the personalities of the crew. Next read copies of the *Journals*, preferably the thirteen-volume set edited by Gary E. Moulton and published by the University of Nebraska Press, of special interest is the Atlas of Clark's excellent maps, or *Journals of Lewis and Clark* edited by Bernard DeVoto. Helpful also is a brilliant piece of cartography produced by Robert M. Bergantino of Montana Tech in Butte, who has detailed their route and campsites on USGS topographic maps. *Along The Trail with Lewis and Clark*, 2nd edition, by Barbara Fifer and Vicky Soderberg is a thorough travel guide to the full course, it will be available in Spring 2002. "Discovering Lewis & Clark" (www.lewis-clark.org), an innovative and informative website produced by Joseph Mussulman, Ph.D. is another excellent reference.

Since the route traverses public as well as private lands, obtaining an understanding of the Montana landscape you'll be traveling through will not only be helpful, but important. In some cases, stretches of the path are not accessible, but the majority of the trip can be seen either by road or water. The land, especially in the Upper Missouri River Breaks National Monument, far eastern Montana and in the southwestern part of the state, has changed little since Lewis and Clark passed through in 1805 and again in 1806. The *Montana Atlas and Gazetteer* is a valuable aid to following our descriptions.

The Lewis & Clark National Historic Trail Interpretive Center in Great Falls, Montana is an absolutely necessary stop either before you commence your own journey or during it. This fascinating, hands-on experience of sight and sound will enrich and enliven your own travels.

Be aware of some of the underlying facts concerning the recorded material. Campsites marked on maps, with few exceptions, are only approximate. During the 200 years that have passed since Meriwether Lewis and William Clark headed west, the course of the Missouri, the "road" they spent much of their time on, has changed, in some instances significantly. Before the dams were built, spring floods, bringing large volumes of water and silt downriver, washed away banks, therefore confluences noted in the Journals might now be two miles away from the present-day locations; also since the dams, many campsites are now under water.

Our campsite location information comes from several sources, including the Robert Bergantino map and various members of the Montana chapters of the Lewis and Clark Trail Heritage Foundation. Some sites were shown to us in the field. We also cross-referenced with Gary Moulton's work, the *Montana Atlas and Gazatteer*, BLM and Forest Service maps and magazine articles. Any errors or omissions in the ensuing manuscript must rest solely on our shoulders and not with those we recruited for advice or referenced.

Clark crossed
the Big Hole
Valley on his
route to the
Yellowstone in
early July 1806.
RICK AND SUSIE GRAETZ

Wild rose
common
along rivers
of Montana's
Great Plains.
RICK AND SUSIE GRAETZ

▸ Cliffs guard
the north side
of the Missouri
River south of
Bainville.
RICK AND SUSIE GRAETZ

For a 120-mile stretch, from Fort Peck through the Charles M. Russell National Wildlife Refuge almost to Fred Robinson Bridge, the Fort Peck Dam has put the majority of their stops beneath the water. Even where the waterways have remained static, or along their cross-country path, many locations can only be guessed. Bergantino has come the closest to anyone in pointing out their approximate locations by studying the explorer's notes and bearings.

Though they seemed to have the instruments to take into consideration the magnetic declination thus keeping errors to a minimum, in a few cases, bearings taken with their compasses could be off ten degrees either way. Overall, information provided in the complete journals as well as the abridged editions is close enough to allow the modern day wanderer to follow the trail with a great deal of enjoyment and a fairly high degree of certainty.

For a long time, the Journals and maps the Captains made were forgotten about, so a good number of the names Lewis and Clark gave to locations have been changed. Fur traders following the Expedition and later homesteaders came up with their own monikers. Most of the written works on Lewis and Clark will point out when today's name for a place differs from the one they gave it.

In Lewis and Clark's era, it was common for words to be spelled phonetically resulting in some interesting variations; Clark especially was a master at this. Therefore, the quotes we have used, with few exceptions, are the way they wrote them. And the quotes were taken from many sources, but most are from the works of Gary Moulton and are used with permission from the University of Nebraska Press.

The purpose of this work is to combine the words of these two explorer/scientists with the geography they passed through as it looks today, and to point would-be-followers in the right direction.

Plan ample time and do the route in segments. Travel slowly, camp where possible and keep your eyes open, for not only will you learn of this epic journey of exploration through our state, but you'll also come to know Montana better.

RICK & SUSIE GRAETZ
Flathead Lake, Montana
September 1, 2001

1805 — The Montana Adventure Begins

Leaving Camp Dubois north of St. Louis on May 14, 1804, Captains Meriwether Lewis and William Clark and the Corps of Discovery arrived at and set up their winter quarters northwest of Bismarck, North Dakota on October 26th, 1804. Christened Fort Mandan, they would spend the next five winter months here, near three Hidatsa (Minnetarrees) and two Mandan Indian villages, putting the finishing touches on their preparations.

Since the Hidatsa warriors made periodic treks to the Rockies and could explain the rivers and mountains yet to be encountered, the explorers interrogated them whenever possible, absorbing as much information as they might about the uncharted territory to the west. To illustrate their knowledge, the natives drew lines representing rivers and trails on tanned skins, on the earth floors of their lodges or in the ashes of fire pits; piles of soil were used to depict elevations above the plain. Clark copied this information onto a map that became one of their most indispensable navigational tools.

From this information, certain key landmarks came to be expected along the way. The first was *"the White Earth River,"* more than 100 miles from Fort Mandan, followed very shortly by the Yellowstone River, or Roche Jaune as the French trappers called it. Further up, the Corps should find, joining the Missouri from the north, *"the river that scolds at all others* (Milk),*"* then from the south *"the Muscle Shell* (Musselshell) *River."* The fifth main landmark was to be a thundering waterfall with an eagle's nest on an island, and close after that, *"the Medicine* (Sun) *River"* coming from the north. They had been told the Missouri would now narrow, enter the mountains and later separate into three distinct branches (Three Forks), the *"north fork"* leading to the Divide.

Frenchman Toussaint Charbonneau, hired as a cook and interpreter for expected contacts with the Indians, had two wives. One, Sacajawea, a young Shoshone 15 or 16 years of age, who, having been kidnapped five years before by the Hidatsa at the Three Forks of the Missouri in Montana, was chosen to accompany her husband and the explorers. The Captains hoped *"the Snake* (Shoshone) *woman,"* as they called her, would be of assistance when meeting her people. This proved to be a wise decision, as she came to be of a far greater value than they had imagined.

In February 1804, only two months before the planned departure, Sacajawea gave birth to a son, Jean Baptiste Charbonneau, nicknamed "Pomp" or "Little Pomp" by the explorers.

Other than the two captains, the party consisted of three sergeants — Gass, Pryor and Ordway, 23 enlisted men all with the rank of private, Clark's black slave — York, Drouillard — a skilled frontiersman and interpreter, Charbonneau, Sacajawea and their son little Baptiste and Lewis's Newfoundland dog Seamen.

The original watercraft that would take the Corps towards the sunset consisted of two pirogues, one white and one red, and six canoes, all shaped out of large cottonwood trees. The pirogues had flat bottoms making them somewhat difficult to control. The canoes were smaller, with curved bottoms and didn't handle very well either. They both had a tendency to take on water, especially when rounding corners into the wind. Poles, oars, ropes, towlines and occasionally a sail were used to move the boats upriver.

▸ Sandstone and yucca, a prairie still-life landscape.
RICK AND SUSIE GRAETZ

"*At this moment, every individual of the party are in good health, and excellent sperits; zealously attatched to the enterprise, and anxious to proceed; not a whisper of discontent or murmur is to be heard among them; but all in unison, act with the most perfect harmoney. With such men I have everything to hope, and but little to fear.*" With these words on April 7, 1805, Lewis, Clark and their crew courageously pushed off against the current heading for a landscape never before seen by white men. Eighteen days later, on April 25th, Meriwether Lewis, traveling over land, reached the confluence of the Missouri and Yellowstone rivers, moving down the checklist of landmarks the Indians had described. While he was investigating a few miles up this new waterway, Clark and his men were still a day behind.

After a late start due to fierce winds, the crew moved west on April 27th into what would become Montana. The night's camp was just west of the North Dakota border and north of today's Nohly. On April 28th, after a fine day under sail with a good wind at their backs and viewing "*great quantities of game,*" they stayed on the south side of the river near Otis Creek.

Several access points are available to view the stretch of the Corps' journey from the North Dakota border to Fort Peck, but it would be best to experience this segment by river. Highway and BLM maps show the few Missouri River crossings and approach roads.

The Mandans and Hidatsa had warned of the ferocious white bear the Expedition would encounter. Lewis took this admonition lightly, assuming that their superior firepower (the natives didn't posses guns) would more than compensate. On April 29th, sometime during midday before

Lewis traveling west by land reached the confluence of the Missouri and Yellowstone rivers on April 25, 1805.
LARRY MAYER

The Missouri River below Culbertson.
RICK AND SUSIE GRAETZ

camping just above today's Big Muddy Creek, Lewis met his first grizzly. He shot the animal, which then pursued him for almost 80 yards before the second bullet killed it. Louis who now gained a new respect for this *"furious and formidable anamal that will frequently pursue the hunter when wounded,"* stated, *"these bear being so hard to die reather intimedates us all; I must confess that I do not like the gentelmen and had rather fight two Indians than one bear."*

It was early spring in Montana and with it came all of the meteorological events common to this time of the year. Strong winds, sometimes blowing at gale force from the west, made it nearly impossible to move at times. Nights could be below freezing and some days brought snow squalls. But typical of spring, many days were pleasant and warm. While the landscape was at it's finest with wildflowers poking through tall green grass and abundant wildlife…deer, bear, antelope, bison, beaver, elk and wolves making their appearance, mosquitoes and the prickly pear cactus proved troublesome.

The men noted seams of coal streaking the banks and sides of buttes, and hills capped with red rocks, today known as scoria, a result of a burning coal vein. Observations of saline seep (salts left behind when water evaporates), *"the banks of the river and sandbars are encrusted with it…and appear perfectly white as if covered with snow or frost,"* plants, berries and birds were detailed.

Continually impressed with the pleasant appearance of the landscape, while camping near Brockton on April 30th, Clark declared, *"the Countrey on both Sides have a butifull appearance."*

May 1st, a particularly nasty storm with waves several feet high caused all forward motion to be halted at noon. The next morning Clark described, *"a verry extroadernaley Climate, to behold the*

22

The Missouri above Snowden looking towards Otis Creek a Lewis/Clark camp of April 28, 1805.
RICK AND SUSIE GRAETZ

trees Green & flowers Spred on the plain & Snow an inch deep." After a late 3pm start, making only about five miles, they camped on the north bank near where Montana Hwy 251 crosses the river.

The crew overnighted at present day Poplar on May 3rd, the Captains named the "*Porcupine (Poplar) River,*" because of the multitude of needled creatures inhabiting the place. While Clark hiked and saw the Little Rocky Mountains far to the west, Lewis penned, "*the country in this neighborhood of this river, and as far as the eye can reach is level, fertile, open and beatifull beyond description.*" They also christened the present Redwater River, "*2000 mile creek,*" estimating it was 2,000 miles from St. Louis.

Making 18 miles on the 4th, Lewis recorded, "*the river bottoms are very extensive…the fore part of this day the river was bordered with timber on both sides, a circumstance that is extreemly rare and the first that has occurred of any thing like the same extent since we left the Mandans…I saw immence quantities of buffaloe in every direction,*" The Corps then traveled another 14 or so miles and spent the evening of May 5th southeast of Wolf Point. Lewis wrote, "*…as usual saw a great quantity of game today…The country is as yesterday beatifull in the extreme.*" As a result of years of river action, the approximate location of this campsite is now more than a mile from the river.

With a favorable wind, the Corps covered a decent 25 miles and camped on May 6th just southwest of the small town of Oswego.

Again praise. "*The country we passed today…is one of the most beautiful plains we have yet seen, it rises gradually from the river bottom…then becoming level as a bowling green…as far as the eye can reach…no appearance of birnt hills coal or pumicestone,*" so noted Lewis of the 15 miles to their encampment of May 7th, a short ways southwest of Frazer.

With a respectable 28 miles behind them, the Corps attained another of the predicted landmarks. Meriwether Lewis, May 8, 1805, "*…the water of this river possesses a peculiar whiteness, being about the colour of a cup of tea with the admixture of a tabelspoonfull of milk. from the colour of it's water we called it Milk river. we think it possible that this may be the river called by the Minitares (Hidatsa) 'the river that scolds at all others'…*" Lewis also noted the Milk River Hills that rise almost 700 feet above the floodplain of the Milk and Missouri. These can be ascended on their south side and reached via MT 24 across Fort Peck Dam. From these points one can view much of the terrain Lewis and Clark described, both along the Missouri on the north side of the hills and southwest out over Fort Peck Lake, once part of the Missouri River channel.

According to their interpretation of information from the Hidatsa, the Rocky Mountains should not be far off; but oh, how wrong they would be. After this momentous day, the resting spot that night was just south of the Milk River confluence and northeast of the town of Fort Peck, Fort Peck Lake and the border of the Charles M. Russell National Wildlife Refuge.

The strong flowing Missouri River Lewis and Clark struggled up for the next two weeks is now stilled by a dam at Fort Peck, transforming the river into a lake covering more than 250,000 acres with 1,600 miles of shoreline. In their time, the Corps plied the shores of a fertile river bottom with "*rich black earth*" and looked up at some of the most spectacular arid landscape in the West. Even today, the deepened waters of the lake have not diminished the topography, now part of the Charles M. Russell National Wildlife Refuge. If we can't follow the exact route, at least we can view what they saw.

Lewis —

"these bear being so hard to die reather intimidates us all; I must confess that I do not like the gentleman and had rather fight two Indians than one bear."

ERWIN AND PEGGY BAUER

Lewis — *"I saw a great
number of feathers
floating down the
river...we did not
perceive from whence
they came, at length we
were surprised by the
appearance of a flock
of Pillican...the number
of which would if
estimated appear
almost in credible."*
ERWIN AND PEGGY BAUER

The mouth of the
Musselshell River on
the Missouri.
LARRY MAYER

Before making camp on the night of May 9th near Duck Creek, the Expedition passed today's Big Dry Arm of Fort Peck Lake, a 40-mile long extension into the badlands south of the Missouri River. Lewis wrote, *"today we passed the bed of the most extraordinary river that I ever beheld. it is as wide as the Missouri is at this place…and not containing a single drop of runing water…we called it Big dry river."*

Ferocious winds continued to plague and slow their advancement on and off for the next several days. By the 11th, they were only southwest of the Pines Recreation Area, and the 13th found them between Crooked Creek Bay and Hell Creek State Park. On the 14th of May, a wild encounter with a seemingly unstoppable grizzly and the near sinking of the white pirogue and subsequent loss of some medicines and important journal notes (most were saved by Sacajawea, who remained the only calm and level headed person in the boat), caused the captains to call for a day to rest and dry out (the 15th) and as Lewis commented, *"we thought it a proper occasion to console ourselves and cheer the sperits of our men and accordingly took a drink of grog and gave each man a gill of sperits."* These two nights were spent a few miles above Snow Creek.

May 17th, that evening, camping just below Seven Blackfoot Creek, *"the party were much harassed"* by a wild fire *"which could not be extinguished."* The next day, after making 21 miles, the Corps passed and camped two miles above Devils Creek Recreation Area.

The big UL Bend of the Missouri where the Corps bedded down on May 19, 1805, is still, in spite of the broadened river, a prominent but low-lying landform. During the day, Clark climbed one of the high buttes nearby and could see the Little Rockies to the northwest and the Musselshell River just beyond the Bend to the south. He may have been atop either Mickey or Brandon butte on the north side of the water.

May 20th brought the voyagers to the southern tip of the UL Bend and the Missouri's meeting with another landmark, *"the Shell river"* or *"Muscle Shell,"* coming in from the south. Lewis recorded *"…it takes it's rise* (origins), *by their* (Hidatsa) *information in the 1st chain of the Rocky mountains at no great distance from the Yellowstone river."* The natives were correct as the Musselshell headwaters in the Castle Mountains to the southwest, less than 100 miles from the Yellowstone.

That night Lewis also wrote, *"…about 5 mi. above the mouth of shell river a handsome river of about 50 yds in width discharged itself on the…upper side; this stream we called Sâh-câ-ger we-âh or bird woman's River after our interpreter the Snake woman."* Over time, this became known as Crooked Creek; but today, in deference to the brave and invaluable service of the young Shoshone woman, it has been rightfully renamed Sacajawea River. Access by land is a road through the Charles M. Russell National Wildlife Refuge, which leads to the Crooked Creek Recreation Area. The mouth of the Musselshell is silting in and will perhaps narrow the Missouri at this point in the future. Today, west of the Musselshell, the lake gradually becomes, once again, a river.

Serious windstorms plagued the Expedition for the next two days; *"we found ourselves so invelloped with clouds of dust and sand that we were could neither cook, eat, nor sleep."* The tired men took refuge the night of the 22nd just below today's CK (or Kannuck) Creek, which they dubbed *"Teapot Creek."*

May 23rd proved to be a day of extremes. Clark's weather report stated, *"a Severe frost last night…the water freeses on the oars. Ice on the edge of the river,"* then later, *"The after part of this*

day was worm & the Misquitors troublesome." Coming upon "a large assemblage of the burrows of the Burrowing Squirrel (prairie dog)" and finding "The wild rose which is now in blume and very abundant," they encamped just before the mouth of Rock Creek, across from the future site of the former steamboat stop and outlaw hangout of Rocky Point. CMR roads access this place on both the north and south.

Early in the morning of May 24, 1805, the party passed "North Mountain creek" (Rock Creek) emanating in the Little Rocky Mountains to the north. With, as Clark mentioned, "This Breeze afforded us good Sailing, the river rising fast. Current verry rapid," one can only imagine them ducking their heads as they "sped" under the then non-existent Fred Robinson Bridge and entered the eastern portion of the Upper Missouri River Breaks National Monument. Making 24 plus miles that day, they retired for the evening at Kendall Bottoms.

The confluence of the Milk and Missouri rivers — to the Indians the Milk was *"the river that scolds at all others."*
LARRY MAYER

The Missouri River at Wolf Point...going west, the Corps passed here on May 5, 1805.
RICK AND SUSIE GRAETZ

▸ The badlands on
the north shore
of Fort Peck
Lake, the waters
of which cover
many of the
Expedition's
campsites.
RICK AND SUSIE GRAETZ

THROUGH THE UPPER MISSOURI RIVER BREAKS NATIONAL MONUMENT

>>——→

Road access to the segment of the Lewis and Clark Expedition, from the Fred Robinson Bridge to Fort Benton, as it moves through the 149 miles of the Upper Missouri River Breaks National Monument, is very limited. So the best way to experience this section is to grab a paddle, plop yourself in a canoe and get out in the middle of it. For those of you who choose to put-in at Fort Benton, Coal Banks or Judith Landing, we have included river miles denoting Lewis and Clark campsites. Since present-day water travelers follow the current downstream (the opposite direction from Lewis and Clark), the river mile numbers in the Monument ascend from Fort Benton (river mile 0) up to Kipp Landing (river mile 149).

On May 24, 1805, the Corps of Discovery settled for the night on the Kendall Bottoms (river mile 146) about three miles upriver from Fred Robinson Bridge and Kipp Landing, and here Captain Clark wrote, *"a cold night...the thermometer Stood this morning at the freesing point...We had a Breeze from the S E which Continued all day."* This campsite can be observed from the Missouri River Back Country Byway road that follows a high ridge west on the south side of the river.

Their May 25th camp (river mile 133) was one mile below the old ferry and the power plant built in the late 1800s to provide energy for mining in the Little Rocky Mountains to the north. Here the Corps killed their first bighorn sheep and provided a minutely detailed description of this animal for their records. The Audubon sheep Lewis and Clark saw were decimated during the early 1900's Homestead Era. Today, a thriving bighorn sheep population frequents the ridges and hillsides of the river. Elk, plentiful in Lewis and Clark's time, are also making a comeback.

On Sunday, May 26th, a site between Bird and Cabin rapids (river mile 114) served as their rest spot. Lewis's journal noted, *"late this evening we passed a very bad rappid...the party had considerable difficulty in ascending it...while they were passing this rappid a female elk and it's fawn swam down through the waves...hence the name of Elk rappids."* However, that title doesn't show on current maps; it would seem that this is today's Bird Rapids.

Earlier the same day, Clark climbed a high point on the north side of the river and saw mountains he mistakenly thought were the main chain of the Rockies. Lewis followed later and showed the uplift to have a compass bearing of N. 65° W. Given their ground position, they were most likely looking at the Bears Paw Mountains, a long way from the desired Rocky Mountains. They had already observed the Little Rockies, another outlier chain, several days earlier. Some accounts mention that the two explorers might have been viewing the Highwoods, but those peaks are to the southwest. Lewis was ecstatic, *"...the rocky Mountains were covered with Snow and the Sun Shone on it in such manner as to give me the most plain and satisfactory view. while I viewed these mountains I felt a secret pleasure in finding myself so near the head of the heretofore conceived boundless Missouri; but when I reflected on the difficulties which this snowey barrier would most probably*

▸ Castle Rock, in the White Rocks section of the Missouri that awed the Corps.
RICK AND SUSIE GRAETZ

The Expedition
pulled in for
the night at the
McGarry Bottoms
on May 27, 1805.
RICK AND SUSIE GRAETZ

Bighorn sheep
were noted along
the Missouri in the
Captains' Journals.
ERWIN AND PEGGY BAUER

throw in my way to the Pacific, and the sufferings and hardships of myself and party in them, it in some measure counterballanced the joy I had felt in the first moments in which I gazed on them; but as I have always held it a crime to anticipate evils I will believe it a good comfortable road untill I am compelled to beleive differently."

The very scenic McGarry Bar (river mile 103), just below the Dauphin Rapids (river mile 102–103), was their camp on May 27th. It is reported in the Journals they experienced troublesome rapids, high winds, heat and scarce wood for their fire. Covering 14 fairly uneventful miles the next day, they found signs of recent Indian habitation along the banks. That night, May 28th, the explorers bedded down about ½ mile below the present Judith Landing Bridge (river mile 88.5), when *"we were all allarmed by a large buffaloe Bull, which swam over from the opposite shore and coming along side of the white perogue, climbed over it to land, he then alarmed ran up the bank at full speed directly towards the fires, and was within 18 inches of the heads of some of the men who lay sleeping before the centinel could allarm him or make him change his course, still more alarmed, he now took his direction immediately towards our lodge, passing between 4 fires and within a few inches of the heads of one range of the men as they yet lay sleeping, when he came near the tent, my dog saved us by causing him to change his course a second time, which he did by turning a little to the right, and was quickly out of sight, leaving us by this time all in an uproar with our guns in our hands, enquiring of each other the cause of the alarm."*

The landscape along the stretch of river from Kendall Bottoms to Judith Landing is much drier appearing than other areas of the Monument. Badland and desert-like topography dominate. The soils consisting of mudstone, silt, clay and sandstone show a myriad of colors with an occasional dark seam of coal separating the layers of sediment. Lewis's notes reflect, *"...the bluffs are composed of irregular tho' horizontal stratas of yellow and brown or black clay, brown and yellowish white sand, of soft yellowish white sandstone and a hard dark brown freestone...this is truly a desert barren country."* Clark described the sector as *"the Deserts of America."* The Missouri Breaks earn their keep here as they create an extensive labyrinth of coulees and canyons that extend outward from the river much further than anywhere else in the Monument.

Judith Landing is a popular take out spot for those who put-in at Coal Banks Landing. Many folks also push off from here to cover the lower part of the Monument. In this area and upstream roughly ten miles, the relief becomes more subdued than it has been below.

On May 29, 1805, passing by the mouth of a *"handsome river"* on the Missouri's south side, just above today's bridge, Captain Clark explored upstream for a short distance and named it for Julia Hancock, whom he hoped to marry. Today it is called the Judith River (river mile 87.5).

A spot on the north side of the Missouri, about a mile up from where the current Arrow River comes in, served as a camp for the Corps that night (river mile 76.5). Lewis also used this same location July 29th, 1806 on his return trip. The stream was christened *"Slaughter River,"* as they had just passed *"the remains of a vast many mangled carcases of Buffalow which had been driven over a precipice of 120 ft. by the Indians and perished; the water appeared to have washed away a part of this immence pile of slaughter and still there remained the fragments of at least a hundred carcases...they created a most horrid stench."*

Further examination of the kill site above their Slaughter River camp reveals, as author Stephen

Looking upriver
towards the
Dauphin Rapids
from above
McGarry
Bottoms.
RICK AND SUSIE GRAETZ

The crew
complained of
rapids here in
the Cow Island
area.
RICK AND SUSIE GRAETZ

Ambrose points out, that the bison, who were known to congregate by the thousands and cross rivers enmasse, probably drowned on their own when the late winter ice gave out. The Indians would have driven the buffalo over a pishkun or precipice with land below it not into the water.

Around river mile 71, a dramatic change in scenery takes place; the scenic white rocks and other spectacular formations begin to appear. This 20-mile extent of river is the best-known length of the journey. Much has been written about it, and Swiss Artist Karl Bodmer, who painted many scenes along the Missouri in 1833, immortalized it.

For most of the way up from Kendall Bottoms, the going had been tough. Turbulent water, strong headwinds, rain and numerous rocks and cliffs that dropped straight to the water stymied their progress; but May 30th was the worst. Clark scrawled, *"more rain has now fallin than we have experienced since the 15th of September last...the wind too high for us to proceed, untill about 11 oClock...banks were So muddey & Slipery that the men could Scercly walk...the day has proved to be raw and Cold."* They advanced only about five miles in all, finding more signs of recent large Indian gatherings, and camped just above the Pablo Islands at river mile 71.3.

Meriwether Lewis had tremendous respect for his men and on May 31st he praised them saying, *"...men are compelled to be in the water even to their armpits, and the water is yet verry could...mud so tenacious they are unable to wear their mockersons...draging the heavy burthen of a canoe and walking...over the sharp fragments of rocks...in short their labour is incredibly painfull and great, yet those fellows bear it without a murmur."* The reward for these trials and tribulations was the magnificent scenery they passed along the way to their camp at the mouth of Eagle Creek (river mile 55.5) and the White Cliffs, considered one of the most beautiful sectors on the Upper Missouri.

In the early morning light, sheer silvery walls and dark towers of rock create stunning reflections on the quiet Missouri's surface. Lewis eloquently stated, *"The hills and river Clifts which we passed today exhibit a most romantic appearance. The bluffs of the river rise to the hight of from two to 300 feet and in most places nearly perpendicular; they are formed of remarkable white sandstone...the water in the course of time in descending from those hills...has trickled down the soft sand clifts and woarn it into a thousand grotesque figures, which with the help a little imagination...are made to represent elegant ranges of lofty freestone buildings, having their parapets well stocked with statuary...As we passed on it seemed as if those seens of visionary inchantment would never have and end...so perfect indeed are those walls that I should have thought that nature had attempted here to rival the human art of masonry had I not recollected that she had first began her work."*

On Sunday, June 1st, they passed Coal Banks Landing (river mile 41.5) at Virgelle and camped 4.5 miles upriver. Lewis noted, *"the river Clifts and bluffs not so high as yesterday and the country becomes more level."* Clark mentioned, *"The roses are in full bloome, I observe yellow berries, red berry bushes Great numbers of Wild or choke Cheries, prickley pares are in blossom & in great numbers."*

June 2nd, Lewis wrote, *"the wind was hard and against us yet we proceded with infinitely more ease than the two precedeing days. The river bluffs still continue to get lower and the plains leveler and more extensive...I think we are now completely above the black hills."* The spot Lewis and Clark camped that evening, beginning a ten-day stay, was at the meeting of the Missouri and Marias rivers (river mile 22). In 1950, a flood diverted the course of the Marias River forcing it to enter the

40

The White Cliffs across from Eagle Creek. May 31, 1805, Lewis — *"The hills and river Clifts which we passed today exhibit a most romantic appearance."*
RICK AND SUSIE GRAETZ

Lewis used the bark of the chokecherry tree to cure a severe ailment that plagued him.
RICK AND SUSIE GRAETZ

Missouri nearly one mile further upstream, thereby altering a physical location in history. The former channel is still visible along the cliffs near the small town of Loma.

Up until June 2, 1805, the information supplied by the Hidatsa Indians to the Expedition proved to be most accurate. On that date however, the Corps encountered something not shown on the crude maps they possessed. The Missouri they had been following for so many months appeared now to split into a north and south fork. The Indians had made no mention of another major waterway coming from the north after the Milk River. They only specified that the explorers would meet a great waterfall, and then soon thereafter the river would enter the mountains. A dilemma of grand proportions was at hand.

Or as one historian aptly stated, *"Lewis and Clark entered what now would be the 'Where in the hell are we?' phase of their Expedition."*

The two leaders were fairly sure the south fork was the Missouri, but the crew was convinced otherwise. Joseph Whitehouse, a member of the Corps, noted in his journal on June 3, *"our officers and all the men differ in their opinions which river to take."* Characteristic of their excellent leadership, the captains agreed to explore both branches so all would be assured.

Lewis on June 3, 1805 scripted, *"to this end an investigation of both streams was the first thing to be done...accordingly we dispatched two light canoes with three men in each up those streams; we also sent out several small parties by land with instructions to penetrate the country as far as they conveniently can permitting themselves time to return this evening and indeavour if possible to discover the distant bearing of those rivers by ascending the rising grounds...Capt. C. & myself stroled out it to the top of the hights in the fork of these rivers from whence we had an extensive and most inchanting view...to the south we saw a range of lofty mountains"* (most likely the Highwoods, east of Great Falls).

The *"top of the hights"* the captains climbed is now marked as Decision Point (river mile 21) and is reached via a dirt road just south of Loma off Hwy 87. Below this spot and closer to the river, the Expedition built caches, storing supplies and the red pirogue, to be retrieved on their homeward journey.

After the return of the scouting parties there was still much uncertainty. It was then decided that to explore further, Clark would follow the south fork and Lewis the north.

June 4, 1805, the two groups separated. It didn't take Clark long to deduce that the south fork was the correct way to go and when he and his men stopped to enjoy a refreshing concoction of spring water and rum, Sergeant Gass named the spot, *"Grog Spring."*

Lewis meanwhile, traveled up the north fork a considerable distance (60 to 70 miles) before coming to the same conclusion. On June 6, 1805 he wrote, *"I now became well convinced that this branch of the Missouri had its direction too much to the north for our rout to the Pacific, and therefore determined to return...having traveled about 25 mes. since noon. it continues to rain and we have no shelter, an uncomfortable nights rest is the natural consequence."*

Trying to return to the camp on the 7th proved to be most difficult as it rained much of the time and they were forced by the uneven landscape to walk along the slippery shores or even at times in the water. Often, in order to make any progress, they had to use their knives to carve hand and footholds in the riverbanks. Lewis may have been the first person to record a mention of gumbo soil. He described the wet earth they were walking on as *"precisely like walking over frozan ground which is thawed to small debth and slips equally as bad."* A potentially fatal mishap owing to the

slicked mud nearly caused both Lewis and a crewmember to slide off a steep precipice. The words scripted that night are as applicable today as they were then, *"we eat a hearty supper...not having taisted a mosel before during the day; I now laid myself down on some willow boughs to a comfortable nights rest, and felt indeed as if I was fully repaid for the toil and pain of the day, so much will a good shelter, a dry bed, and comfortable supper revive the sperits of the waryed and hungry traveler."*

So assured that the river he was following was not the Missouri, on June 8th Lewis named it Maria's River for his cousin. Misery forgotten, he expounded poetically, *"it is a noble river...it passes through a rich fertile and one of the most beautifully picturesque countries that I ever beheld...inumerable herds of living animals are seen, it's borders garnished with one continued garden of roses, while its lofty and open forests, are the habitation of miriads of the feathered tribes who salute the ear of the passing traveler with their wild and simple, yet sweet and cheerfull melody.— I arrived at camp about 5 Oclock in the evening much fatigued, where I found Capt. Clark and the balance of the party waiting our return with some anxiety for our safety"*

In spite of the conclusions reached by their leaders, the men still felt strongly the north fork was the correct route. Yet even though *"Cruzatte who had been an old Missouri navigator and who from his integrity knowledge and skill as a waterman had acquired the confidence of every individual of the party declared it as his opinion that the N. Fork was the true genuine Missouri and could be no other,"* the crew all stated they would willingly and *"very cheerfully"* follow the captains. The decision then was made for Lewis and a small party to advance by land and Clark to bring the rest of the Expedition upriver.

Looking near Kendall Bottoms — the Expedition's May 24, 1805 camp.
RICK AND SUSIE GRAETZ

Above the Brulé Bottoms looking towards the Bears Paw Mountains.
RICK AND SUSIE GRAETZ

The morning of June 11, 1805, Lewis and his men struck out across the land making only about nine miles to somewhere in the vicinity of Vimy Ridge (river mile 8.2), the former Indian route to Fort Benton, also known as Cracon du Nez. Lewis had severe intestinal pain and made a bitter medicine with chokecherry twigs boiled in water from the same *"Grog Spring"* used by Clark the past June 4th. The remedy worked, and the next day he and his men covered 27 miles.

Clark's advance upstream was somewhat slower. Leaving camp on the 12th, they stayed at Lewis's previous night's spot (river mile 8.2) just downstream from Fort Benton (river mile 0). Clark worried, *"the Interpreters woman verry Sick worse than She has been. I give her medison."*

The last half of the Expedition passed out of today's Monument boundary on June 13, 1805, when Clark's party struggled five miles beyond Fort Benton to their night's camp. Clark noted, *"one man Sick & 3 with Swellings, the Indian woman verry Sick."*

Meanwhile, that same day, Meriwether and his advance party finally hit paydirt. Exclaiming, *"whin my ears were saluted with the agreeable sound of a fall of water and advancing a little further I saw the spray arrise above the plain like a collumn of smoke...which soon began to make a roaring too tremendous to be mistaken for any cause short of the great falls of the Missouri,"* Lewis clambered down a steep cliff in order *"to gaze on this is sublimely grand specticle...the grandest sight I ever beheld."* The first known white man to view this scene then sent word to *"Clark and the party of my success in finding the falls and settle in their minds all further doubts as to the Missouri."*

The Great Falls

>> —>

Struck by a feeling of complete inadequacy to put into words the power and splendor of the sight before him, Lewis wished for the talent of an artist *"that I might be enabled to give to the enlightened world some just idea of this truly magnificent and sublimely grand object...to give the world some faint idea of an object which at this moment fills me with such pleasure and astonishment, and which of it's kind I will venture to ascert is second to but one in the known world."* Being so overwhelmed, he set camp on the bank below the Great Falls. Today, Ryan Dam has greatly diminished the spectacle he witnessed.

Up at sunrise on June 14, 1805, Lewis, after giving the day's orders to his men, shouldered his gun and espontoon and headed off alone to scout the river above the falls. A quick five miles brought him to an unexpected second water cascade he named Crooked Falls. Then being led by *"a tremendous roaring above me,"* Lewis was assaulted by the scene of another *"great cataract"* that *"rivals for glory"* the one *"which I had discovered yesterday."* This once glorious Rainbow Falls has been robbed of much of her splendor by the construction of Rainbow Dam. Almost immediately, Lewis stumbled onto another waterfall (no longer visible); becoming jaded he explained, *"in any other neighborhood but this, such a cascade would probably be extolled for it's beaty and magnifficence, but here I passed it by with but little attention...At a distance of 2½ miles I arrived at another cataract of 26 feet...below this falls at a little distance a beautiful little Island...is situated about the middle of the river. In this Island on a Cottonwood tree an Eagle has placed her nest."* Another landmark achieved. The falls, complete with the noble bird's abode, just as the Hidatsa had described it!

The present-day name came more than 70 years later when Thomas P. Roberts, a railway engineer doing survey work, was nearly attacked by a black eagle while viewing the falls. Upon noticing the bird's nest in a cottonwood tree on an island below the thundering curtain of water, he recalled Lewis's mention of the same, and thought it fitting to christen the site Black Eagle Falls.

Somehow, something had gotten lost in the translation at Fort Mandan. Initially, from the information given by the Hidatsa, the captains assumed there would be just one falls and that it would only take half a day to get around it. With a total of five major falls each separated by rapids, obviously the portage was going to take much longer.

In order to better understand the portage and all other aspects of the Expedition, stop and visit the remarkable Lewis and Clark National Historic Trail Interpretive Center in Great Falls (on River Drive near Giant Springs State Park 406-727-8733). Information and advice on how best to experience and view the numerous local Lewis and Clark historic places is up-to-date and readily available here. Access to an extensive archival library, book store, hundreds of brochures covering the entire route, movie presentation, living history site, interactive displays, knowledgeable tour guides and interpretive trails are all included in the admission fee.

Climbing the highest hill behind Black Eagle Falls, Lewis observed another large river flowing in four miles to the west. *"after feasting my eyes on this ravishing prospect and resting myself a few minutes I determined to procede...convinced that it was the river the Indians call 'medicine (Sun)'*

>> *"whin my ears were saluted with the agreeable sound of a fall of water,"* Lewis knew he had reached the *"great falls of the Missouri,"*

RICK AND SUSIE GRAETZ

44

which they informed us fell into the Missouri just above the falls." On his way to investigate, he had a near-fatal encounter with a grizzly, then *"returning through the level bottom of Medicine (Sun) river and about 200 yards distant from the Missouri"* met up with and fired on a *"tyger cat"*-like animal (probably a wolverine) *"looking immediately at me as if it designed to spring on me...it now seem to me that all the beasts of the neighbourhood had made a league to distroy me...for I had not proceded more than three hundred yards...before three bull buffaloe...ran full speed towards me."*

Captain Clark, with an extremely ill Sacajawea on board, slowly battled the natural obstacles Mother Nature continued to throw in his and his men's path. On the 16th of June, he halted below the mouth of *"portage (Belt) creek,"* setting up what would become the base camp for their month-long assault around the Great Falls.

As part of Lewis's effort to cure Sacajawea, who had been exceptionally sick for several days, he used the water of a sulphur spring that is located yet today across the river from the mouth of Belt Creek.

It is possible to visit the Sulphur Spring by taking the rough trail from Moroney Dam along the river's edge for about one mile. The path ends a mile or so further at a fenceline, designating private land. From this fence, the site of the Lower Portage Camp may be glimpsed looking downriver towards a wide flat spot on the opposite shore.

By the 20th, considering their own observations as well as reports from the men who had been sent to explore, it was determined that the best portage route would be up on the prairie to the south of the river, a total distance of about 18 miles. The Upper Portage Camp, was situated just to the south of Great Falls across from the White Bear Islands, a name Clark gave to the place owing to the many grizzlies inhabiting them. When Lewis and Clark came through this country, these giant creatures were still a prairie animal. The islands not only served up a feast of washed up buffalo carcasses for the bears, but the sand was soft, enabling them to excavate winter dens alongside the cottonwood trees.

The site of the Upper Portage Camp is yet visible today, although time has silted in the channel that existed between it and the island they used for storage. Today, the former riverbed is a very obvious depression running through a hay field. A lone cottonwood stands on the edge of what was once the riverbank.

It was decided that Lewis would portage first in order to commence work on his invention, the collapsible, lightweight, iron boat frame. Clark would remain and command the subsequent transfers. By now, after constant doctoring from Lewis, Sacajawea had recovered and was regaining her strength, the wheels and truck frames needed to transport the canoes overland were completed and the men eager to get underway.

June 22, 1805, the first portage attempt was fraught with broken axels and several destroyed wheel parts, but by nightfall they had arrived at the White Bear Islands. The route went up Belt Creek 1¾ miles, turned south and eventually southwest crossing Willow Run, currently called Box Elder Creek. From there it passed through the center of today's Malmstrom Air Force Base, skirted the southeast corner of the city and on to the Upper Portage Camp. Lewis started working on the iron boat the next day.

Portaging proved to be one of the most demanding undertakings the Corps of Discovery experienced. In describing the grueling task of moving the wooden boats up the sides of steep ravines and

46

▸▸ Lower Portage
Camp, used
from June 16–
July 2, 1805,
just below the
mouth of Belt
Creek.
RICK AND SUSIE GRAETZ

across the prickly pear cactus covered ground, Clark wrote, "...*the men has to haul with all their strength...maney times every man all catching the grass & knobes & stones with their hands to give them more force in drawing their Canoes & Loads...maney limping from the Soreness of their feet...but no man Complains...all go Cheerfully on — to State the fatigues of this party would take up more of the journal than other notes which I find Scercely time to Set down.*" Lewis also noted that "*at every halt, these poor fellows tumble down and are so much fortiegued that many of them are asleep in an instant...others faint and unable to stand for a few minutes.*"

As if the labor wasn't difficult enough, at least one if not a combination of "*Musquetoes,*" heat, intense winds, torrential rain, lightning and hail "*so large and driven with such force as...that it nocked many of them down...most of them were bleeding freely,*" confronted the party almost daily as they ferried the baggage and canoes.

On the 29th, Clark, Charbonneau, Sacajawea and her son had taken refuge in a coulee when a severe hail and rain storm hit. A flash flood tearing through the bottom almost drowned them all; it was a narrow escape thanks to the captain's quick action. The next day, Capt. Clark assured Lewis he had seen at least ten thousand buffalo all at once grazing along the river.

The move around the falls began on June 22nd. By the 2nd of July, the last of the baggage was delivered to the upper camp, but Lewis's experimental boat had yet to be completed.

48

The portage route looking towards Box Elder Creek and the Little Belt Mountains.
RICK AND SUSIE GRAETZ

49

Water from
Sacajawea
Springs, across
from Belt Creek,
helped bring the
Shoshone
woman back
to health.
RICK AND SUSIE GRAETZ

Great Falls,
Montana
RICK AND SUSIE GRAETZ

In Search Of
The Three Forks Of The Missouri

With the portage of the falls completed on July 2, 1805, the more valuable time was now needed to finish building, as the men called it, Lewis's *"Experiment,"* the light weight, collapsible, iron boat frame the party had been carrying for this very occasion.

With no pine trees in the area from which to secure the pitch or tar needed to seal the seams of the 28 elk and three buffalo hides the men had sewn together to cover the frame, Lewis wrote on July 4th, *"no appearance of tar yet and I am now confident that we shall not be able to obtain any; a serious misfortune. I employed a number of hands on the boat today and by 4 P M. in the evening completed her except the most difficult part of the work that of making her seams secure."*

Time was passing quickly, they had been engaged in the construction of the iron boat since the 23rd of June and an alternative recipe for waterproofing the hull was yet to be found. Despite the past hardships, the present frustrations and the uncertain future, Lewis, commenting on the commitment and courage of his men, writes, *"all appear perfectly to have made up their minds to suceed in the expedition or purish in the attempt. we all beleive that we are now about to enter on the most perilous and difficult part of our voyage, yet I see no one repining; all appear ready to met those difficulties which wait us with resolution and becoming fortitude."* What a marvelous testament to the leadership qualities of Lewis and Clark.

As a day of national celebrating on July 4th, and *"our work being at an end this evening, we gave the men a drink of sperits, it being the last of our stock, and some of them appeared a little sensible of it's effects…the fiddle was plyed and they danced very merrily until 9 in the evening when a shower of rain put an end to that part of the amusement tho' they continued their mirth with song and festive jokes and were extreemly merry until late at night. We had a very comfortable dinner, of bacon, beans, suit dumplings & buffaloe beaf &c. in short we had no just cause to covet the sumptuous feasts of our countrymen on this day."*

On July 5th, desperate for a concoction to seal the craft, Lewis worried, *"This morning I had the boat removed to an open situation, scaffold her off the ground, turned her keel to the sun and kindled fires under her to dry her more expediciously. I then set a couple of men to pounding of charcoal to form a composition with some beeswax which we have and buffaloe tallow now my only hope and resource for paying my boat; I sincerely hope it may answer yet I fear it will not. the boat in every other rispect completely answers my most sanguine expectation."*

For the next several days, the men made and repaired clothing, hunted, continued working on the boat and in general prepared for the next segment of their forward movement. July 9th, the iron vessel was completed, and that afternoon *"we corked the canoes and put them in the water and also launched the boat, she lay like a perfect cork on the water. five men would carry her with the greatest ease."* How proud and relieved Captain Lewis must have felt at that moment. Then as the men

The Corps of Discovery first entered the mountains several miles upriver from present-day Cascade.
JOHN LAMBING

began loading the canoes, *"a violent wind commenced and...continued violent untill late in the evening."* Upon examining the iron boat, they found *"she leaked in such manner that she would not answer. I need not add that this circumstance mortifyed me not a little; and to prevent her leaking without pich was impossible with us, and to obtain this article was equally impossible, therefore the evil was irreparable...but to make any further experiments in our present situation seemed to me madness; the buffaloe had principally dserted us, and the season was now advancing fast. I therefore relinquished all further hope of my favorite boat...and deposite the iron fraim at this place as it could probably be of no further service to us...I bid a dieu to my boat, and her expected services."*

It was now necessary to build two canoes to carry the surplus baggage. Luckily, on a previous hunting excursion, the men had found *"trees sufficiently a large for this purpose might be obtained in a bottom...about 8 miles distant by land."* And so it was, on the morning of July 10th, 1805, Captain Clark and ten men, struck out overland to what became known as the "Canoe Camp." Situated on the north side of the river, southeast of Antelope Butte and about five miles east of the town of Ulm as the prairie falcon flies, it was "home" for the four days and five nights it took to make the canoes. Today, the site still holds enormous cottonwood trees, some estimated to date back to lewis and Clark's time.

On July 13th, Lewis made the following entry from the Canoe Camp, *"The Musquetoes and knats are more troublesome here if possible than they were at the White bear Islands...it is impossible to sleep a moment without being defended against the attacks of these most tormenting of all insects."*

The next part of their journey took them through a transition zone from the prairie across big valleys into the mountains themselves. Much of their route from here to the Three Forks can be seen from the road. Interstate-15 and side roads parallel the path on water and land for much of the way. Where their course veers from the roadway, it's possible to boat up and down the Missouri and the lakes it now forms. When the trail enters the Prickly Pear Valley and Helena, roads once more approximate much of the distance south.

With Captain Clark in charge of the boats, Lewis describes the events of July 15th. *"We arrose very early this morning, assigned the canoes their loads...we now found our vessels eight in number all heavily laden...10A.M. we once more saw ourselves fairly under way much to my joy...I continued my walk all the evening...we passed the entrance of a beautifull river 80 yards wide which falls in on the Lard. side which in honour of Mr. Robert Smith the Secretary of the Navy we called Smith's River.* (The Smith reaches the Missouri near Ulm) *this stream meanders through a most lovely valley to the S. E. for about 25 miles when it enters the Rocky mountains and is concealed from our view...we have now passed Fort Mountain* (Square Butte southwest of Ulm that Charlie Russell used in so many of his paintings) *on our right it appears to be about ten miles distant...the prickly pear is now in full blume and forms one of the beauties as well as the greatest pests of the plains. the sunflower is also in blume and is abundant. this plant is common to every part of the Missouri from it's entrance to this place."* Their camp for the night was a few miles upriver from Ulm.

Throughout the Expedition, Meriwether Lewis made many notes on the landscape, plants and wildlife; he mentioned the *"shining Mountains"* to the west, explaining that the sun glancing off of the snow gave the mountains a *"glittering appearance."* Native Americans and later, pioneers head-

Charlie Russell Square Butte known as *"Fort Mountain,"* to the Corps, southwest of Great Falls.
RICK AND SUSIE GRAETZ

Lewis, of the prickly pear cactus — *"one of the beauties as well as the greatest pests of the plains."*
RICK AND SUSIE GRAETZ

▸ A drift boat
works the
currents of
the Missouri
downriver
from Craig.
RICK AND SUSIE GRAETZ

ing west across the Montana prairie and modern day travelers have all called the Rocky Mountain Front *"the land of the shining mountains."*

July 16th, the Corps found evidence of Indian presence that *"appeared to have been deserted about 10 days; we supposed that they were snake Indians...this appearance gives me much hope of meeting with these people shortly...we pursued our rout through a high roling plain to a rappid immediately at the foot of the mountain where the Missouri first enters them and seems to be closely hemned in by the mountains on both sides...at this place there is a large rock Of 400 feet high wich stands immediately in the gap which the missouri makes on its passage from the mountains...this rock I called the tower. it may be ascended with some difficulty nearly to it's summit, and from it there is a most pleasing view of the country we are now about to leave."*

The Tower is visible today immediately upon exiting I-15 at Hardy Creek. Lewis's camp that night was near the Hardy Bridge on the west side of the river. The Adel Mountains were to the east and a series of broken hills and buttes stretched out toward the west. Clark and his men bedded down approximately four miles by road past Cascade, near a spot along the river called Barrets. On July 17th, the two groups met and camped about a mile below the entrance of the Dearborn River, which they named in honor of the Secretary of War. The Frontage Road, just down from the Dearborn boat launch, passes the bend in the river where they spent the night. Again the captains split up, this time with Clark on land and Lewis staying with the canoes.

Clark noted on July 18th, *"we thought it prudent for a partey to go a head for fear our fireing Should allarm the Indians and cause them to leave the river and take to the mountains for Safty from their enemes who visit them thro this rout. I deturmined to go a head with a Small partey a few days and find the Snake Indians if possible...we Camped on a Small run of Clear Cold water, musquitors verry troublesom the forepart of the evening."*

According to Lewis and Clark scholar and mapmaker Robert Bergantino, *"Clark probably left the Missouri River near Holter Dam and continued south-southeast to Falls Gulch. He then followed that gulch to Towhead Gulch and down that to Hilger Valley. Clark's camp appears to be south of the summit of the pass on Towhead Gulch about two miles west of Beartooth Mountain (The Sleeping Giant)."*

Lewis in the mean time was maneuvering up the Missouri through a winding, mixed terrain of canyons and narrow valleys. His camp on the 18th was somewhere in the vicinity of the center of today's Lower Holter Lake, easily reached from the towns of either Craig or Wolf Creek.

On July 19th, Lewis's contingent was passing through today's very popular Gates of the Mountains Recreation Area, which extends between Lower Holter and Holter lakes. It skirts through the northern edge of the Beartooth Game Range and the Gates of the Mountains Wilderness. Roads extend towards the game sanctuary from the east side of Lower Holter Lake and then trails lead to some of the higher ridges and points. Most people view this area by water.

In Lewis's words, *"The Musquetoes are very troublesome to us as usual...whever we get a view of the lofty summits of the mountains the snow presents itself, altho we are almost suffocated in this confined vally with heat...this evening we entered much the most remarkable clifts that we have yet seen. these clifts rise from the waters edge on either side perpendicularly to the hight of about 1200 feet. every object here wears a dark and gloomy aspect. the towering and projecting rocks in many*

Several of the
Expedition's camps
were along the segment
of the Missouri now
under the waters of
Canyon Ferry Lake.
RICK AND SUSIE GRAETZ

Clark stayed on land and
west of the Missouri as
he made his way through
this area north of Toston.
RICK AND SUSIE GRAETZ

*"from the singular
appearance of this place
I called it the gates of the
rocky mountains."*
Lewis, August 19, 1806.
RICK AND SUSIE GRAETZ

places seem ready to tumble on us…for the distance of 5 3/4 miles…the river appears to have woarn a passage just the width of it's channel or 150 yds. it is deep from side to side nor is ther in the 1st 3 miles of this distance a spot…on which a man could rest the soal of his foot…it happens fortunately that altho the current is strong it is not so much so but what it may be overcome with the oars for there is hear no possibility of using either the cord or Setting pole. it was late in the evening before I entered this place and was obliged to continue my rout untill sometime after dark before I found a place sufficiently large to encamp my small party…from the singular appearance of this place I called it the gates of the rocky mountains." During the summer, there is an a interpretive tour by boat from Holter Lake through the "Gates."

When Lewis halted here, just inside the prominent opening of the canyon to Holter Lake on the south side of the river, there was apparently a sliver of shore to camp on; today the water level, raised by Holter Dam, extends to the walls of the limestone cliffs.

Clark in the mean time followed an old Indian road, which took him from the Sieben Flats area past the Hilger Ranch to the south end of Holter Lake, there he crossed the hilly lands to the east of today's North Pass on I-15 and traversed the east side of Lake Helena where he *"passed a hansome valley watered by a large creek* (Ordway Creek to them and now Prickly Pear Creek, which connects Lake Helena to Hauser Lake),*"* resting for the night near today's Lakeside on Hauser Lake.

Leaving the impressive Gates of the Mountains on the 20th, Lewis describes *"…the hills re- treated from the river and the valley became wider than we have seen since we entered the moun- tains."* Noticing a column of smoke coming from a nearby valley, *"we were at a loss to determine whether it had been set on fire by the natives as a signall among themselves on discovering us, as is their custom or whether it had been set on fire by Capt. C. and party accidentally. the first however proved to be the fact."* Once more the elusive quarry disappears. *"in the evening…we encamped on the Lard. side near a spring on a high bank the prickly pears are so abundant that we could scarcely find room to lye. just above our camp the river is again closed in by the Mouts. on both sides."* Lewis's camp was about ½ mile below the bridge crossing Hauser Lake on Route 280 to York and can be seen from the bridge.

In departing his camp of the 20th below Spokane Creek on Hauser Lake, *"Capt. Clark set out early and proceeded on through a valley leaving the river about six miles to his left; he fell in with an old Indian road which he pursued untill it struck the river about 18 miles from his camp of the last evening just above the entrance of a large creek which we call white paint Creek.* (probably Beaver Creek, midway down the west side of Canyon Ferry Lake)…*the party were so much fortiegued with their march and their feet cut with the flint and perced with the prickly pears untill they had become so painfull that he proceeded but liitle further before he determined to encamp on the river and wait my arrival."*

The captains were now entering a landscape of broad valleys and big mountains that character- ize southwest Montana. Lewis's water route snaking through alternating narrow canyons of the Missouri to open meadows, passed American Bar along Holter Lake and White Sandy and Black Sandy beaches and the entrance to Prickly Pear Creek, all on Hauser Lake. Clark came in direct touch with today's Prickly Pear Valley, the first of the big intermountain valleys they would encoun- ter, and the site of Montana's future capital. From here they would travel through the area now

covered by Canyon Ferry Lake, a wide valley in itself that stretches northeast to the Big Belt Mountains and southwest to the Elkhorns. Nearly all of this post-portage piece of their journey can be experienced by various systems of roads to, or on the water from, the Three Forks, the next major landmark they were seeking.

The July 21, 1805 Journal notes for Lewis include *"...this morning we passed a bold creek...this we called Pryor's Creek* (Spokane Creek) *after Sergt. Pryor one of our party."* The camp was about five miles above Canyon Ferry Dam and on the east side of the Spokane Hills. It would have been close to where Avalanche Creek entered the Missouri River on its west side.

Lewis and his men received good news on the 22nd of July when *"the Indian woman recognizes the country and assures us that this is the river on which her relations live, and that the three forks are at no great distance. this peice of information has cheered the sperits of the party who now begin to console themselves with the anticipation of shortly seeing the head of the missouri yet unknown to the civilized world."* Still on Canyon Ferry Lake, Lewis meets up with the sore-footed Clark. The united group paddles its way upstream a few miles above Beaver Creek, camping on the left side of the river near an island. The campsites of the past two days are now under the waters of Canyon Ferry Lake.

Clark, determined to continue on foot in search of the Shoshone even though he was nearly crippled, followed an Indian road (still faintly visible) and spent the evening of July 23rd about four miles below Toston along the river. The same day, Lewis met Duck Creek where it entered the Missouri and named it *"Whitehous's Creek after Josph. Whitehouse one of the party."* His camp that night was at the upper end of Canyon Ferry Lake probably in the area of the man-made bird nesting islands north of Townsend.

Early in the morning of the 24th, Lewis and his men *"passed a remarkable bluff of a crimson coloured earth on Stard. intermixed with Stratas of black and brick red slate."* These are now called the Crimson Bluffs and are about a mile southwest of Townsend. From above them one can look up the main street of Townsend. On private ground, efforts are underway to have them purchased for public ownership. Lewis spent the night about six miles further, most likely south of Yorks Islands in the area of Dry Creek. The islands in the area, which until recently was named Deepdale, a fishing access site, are now Yorks Islands in honor of Clark's servant York. Drawing them on his map, the captain viewed them from atop a high hill. River Road out of Townsend skirts this vantage point on its east side.

Clark traveled across the Crow Creek valley where they spotted a horse, and camped that night about 16 air miles south of Lewis, in the broken hills and ridges along the Missouri, below Trident just short of the Three Forks.

Heading towards and then past Toston on the 25th, Lewis relates that *"...the face of the country...were the same as yesterday's, untill late in the evening, when the valley appeared to termineate and the river was again hemned in on both sides with high caiggy and rocky clifts* (to Clark this area was *"Little Gate of the Mountain"* it is between Lombard and Toston) *soon after entering these hills or lower mountains we passed a number of fine bold springs which burst out underneath the Lard (left) clifts...we passed a large Crk. today in the plain country...this stream we called Gass's Creek* (Crow Creek coming from the Elkhorn Mountains). They spent the night south of Toston near

Lewis, July 24, 1805, we *"passed a remarkable bluff of a crimson coloured earth,"* the Crimson Bluffs west of Townsend.
RICK AND SUSIE GRAETZ

Toston Dam. The next day they named a small waterway *"Howard's* (Sixteenmile) *Creek"* after another one of their men.

Finally on July 25, 1805 Captain Clark proclaims, *"a fine morning we proceeded on a fiew miles to the three forks of the Missouri."* On the morning of July 27th, Lewis and his men met up with Clark at the Three Forks.

Now a new phase of the Corps of Discovery's adventure was about to start. They still hadn't found the Shoshone and were getting more anxious about it each day.

To Lemhi Pass And The Shoshone Camp

On the morning of July 25, 1805, the advance party of the Expedition reached the last of the expected landmarks. Captain Clark, in spite of feet painfully blistered and ravaged with prickly pear thorns, was traveling overland and a couple of days ahead of Lewis, when he arrived at *"the three forks of the Missouri."* Quickly choosing to explore the *"North fork"* (soon to be named Jefferson's River), which in his estimation, was the route to the Columbia, he left a note for Lewis and spent the next two days in search of the Shoshone Indians. Contracting *"a high fever & akeing in all my bones,"* and finding no sign of the Natives, he reluctantly turned back, crossed over to the middle fork and camped for the night explaining *"...I continue to be verry unwell fever verry high."*

Clark spent the nights of July 25th–26th at two separate camps on *"Philosophy River (Willow Creek)"* near the present town of Willow Creek.

Arriving at the meeting of the rivers on July 27th Lewis stated, *"the country opens suddonly to extensive and beatifull plains and meadows which appeared to be surrounded in every direction with distant and lofty mountains; supposing this to be the Three Forks of the Missouri I halted the party."* Lewis then walked about ½ mile up the Gallatin and *"ascended the point of a high limestone clift (Lewis's Rock) from whence I commanded a most perfect view of the neighbouring country."* The explorer was beholding the Spanish Peaks and Madison Range to the south, the Gallatin range to the southeast and the Tobacco Root Mountains in his southwest view field. He could also see the Bridger Range directly to the east. In between was the lush, wide valley of the Gallatin River.

Take the I-90 exit at Three Forks and follow the signs to MT 286 and the Missouri Headwaters State Park. Here at the actual forks of the Missouri is a wonderful complex of picnic, interpretive, camping and fishing accesses. It is exciting to stand on the bridge over the Gallatin River and look across, or walk the path down to the point where the waters of the now combined Jefferson/Madison River come together with the Gallatin. And from there on down, it's the Missouri.

Lewis called for the canoes to be unloaded; several of the men went in search of fresh meat and the rest *"are busily engaged in dressing their skins, making mockersons, lexing (leggings) &c to make themselves comfortable."* Clark and his men stumbled into camp. Taking in to consideration the exhausted condition of the crew and Clark's destroyed feet *"and indisposition, was a further inducement for my remaining here a couple of days...we begin to feel considerable anxiety with rispect to the Snake Indians. if we do not find them or some other nation who have horses I fear the successfull issue of our voyage will be very doubtfull."*

Good news came as Sacajawea recognized the area and informed them that this was the exact place her people were encamped when the Hidatsa raid occurred five years earlier. And where, after trying to escape, she had been captured some three to four miles away towards the town of Three Forks.

There was no question in the two leaders' minds that this was the headwaters of the Mighty Missouri. July 28th, Lewis wrote, *"Both Capt. C. and myself corrisponded in opinion, with rispect, to the impropriety of calling either of these streams the Missouri and accordingly agreed to name*

▸ Here the combined flows of the Jefferson, Madison and Gallatin rivers at Three Forks initiate the Missouri and send it on it's way to the Mississippi.
LARRY MAYER

them...we called the S. W. Fork, that which we meant to ascend, Jefferson's river in honor of Thomas Jefferson. the Middle fork we called Madison's River in honor of James Madison, and the S. E. Fork we called Gallitin's river in honor of Albert Gallitin."

To continue following the trail, get back on Hwy 287 from I-90 and follow the Jefferson River to the southwest.

On July 30th, the party set out again, this time Clark, who was *"still very languid and complains of a general soarness in all his limbs,"* traveled by water, while Lewis went ahead on land *"in search of the Snake Indians."* Following a trail over the mountains on the north side of the Jefferson, he trekked through the same high points that hold the Lewis and Clark Caverns. Both captains continually commented on the uncompromising heat, the *"troublesome Musquetoes"* and the *"emence number of beaver and orter in this little river."* After a particularly arduous day, Clark and the party halted near *"Philosophy River (Willow Creek),"* Lewis spent the night alone about two miles above them on an island awaiting the canoes.

July 31, 1805, Lewis summed up the day, *"the mountains on both side of the river at no great distance are very lofty. we have a lame crew just now,"* and camped that night at the mouth of Antelope Creek several miles above the Sappington Bridge and downstream from the Lewis and Clark Caverns (which they did not come across). Subsequent entries mentioned how he was *"determined to go in search of the Snake Indians."* State Route 2 now takes over to La Hood through Whitehall, then State Route 55 to Silver Star.

Arriving at *"a mountain through which a river passes,"* Lewis, doggedly fighting heat, thirst and *"tremendous clifts of ragged and nearly perpendicular rocks,"* camped on the 1st of August above Cardwell. The same night, Clark, making slow progress with the canoes, stayed just downstream near La Hood, at the meeting of today's Boulder River and the Jefferson. The two waterways near here were labeled after members of the Expedition; the Boulder — *"Field's Creek"* after Reuben Field and the South Boulder Creek at Cardwell — *"Frazer's Creek"* after Robert Frazer.

Passing between the Tobacco Root Mountains on the east and the Highlands to the West on August 2nd, Lewis described, *"the tops of these mountains were yet partially covered with snow while we in the valley. were suffocated nearly with the intense heat of the midday sun. the nights are so could that two blankets are not more than sufficient covering."* This day they christened the present Whitetail Creek by the town of Whitehall — *"Birth Creek"* in honor of Clark's 35th birthday the day before. Lewis camped that night in the heart of the valley at Waterloo, just above Silver Star.

After *"having traveled by estimate 23 miles,"* Lewis's August 3rd camp was near the mouth of the *"Wisdom (Big Hole) river."* Clark's men, two days in arrears and still struggling up the Jefferson with the canoes and supplies, *"wer compelled to be a great proportion of their time in the water today; they have had a severe days labour and are much fortiegued."*

A missed communication caused Captain Clark to lose precious time and energy investigating the Big Hole River. On August 4th, Lewis left a note for Clark on a green willow pole *"recommending his taking the middle fork (Jefferson)."* The next day, due to the possible intervention of an errant beaver, Clark failed to see the missive and turned up the Big Hole River only to be stopped about a mile in, by brush so thick *"they were obliged to cut a passage through."* They spent a

Tobacco Root Mountains rise above the Jefferson Valley near Silver Star.
RICK AND SUSIE GRAETZ

Going against the current, rocks and rapids of the Jefferson made progress difficult for the explorers.
RICK AND SUSIE GRAETZ

▸ From Lewis's
Rock at Three
Forks looking
up the Gallatin
Valley.
RICK AND SUSIE GRAETZ

▸ The Beaverhead
Valley and the
"hogback"
Lewis climbed
when he
explored the
Big Hole River.
RICK AND SUSIE GRAETZ

CAMP FORTUNATE

The Lewis and Clark Expedition, of 1804-180 reaches of the Louisiana Purchase to establi Pacific Northwest. Few points along the significance of Camp Fortunate or Two Forks waters of Clark Canyon Reservoir, Capt. Lewis, trail in advance of the expedition's main party, junction of Red Rock River and Horse Prairie Cre 1805. Two days later he crossed the Continental Divide at Lemhi P and met Shoshoni Indians. On August 17th, Lewis rejoined Clark an at this site where they camped with the Shoshoni Indians until Augu meeting, expedition interpreter Sacagawea, also a Shoshoni, was reu brother Cameahwait, whom she had not seen in five years. Through h Clark negotiated for horses — all important for the expedition's trip acro tains to the Columbia River drainage. Here, too, expedition members ca and supplies for their return. William Clark revisited this point in July empty the cache and begin the trip down the Missouri to St. Louis. The the name "Fortunate" for the meeting with the Indians, and the important from water to overland travel. The actual valley where the reservior is t called "Service berry vallie", and Horse Prairie they designated "Shoshon

Site of the now underwater Camp Fortunate, where Lewis and Clark traded with the Shoshone for horses.
RICK AND SUSIE GRAETZ

miserable, wet night on a flooded island and were reunited with Lewis the next day, August 6th, camping across from the Big Hole's confluence. At this point, the Expedition was about to enter the waters of the Beaverhead River.

In exploring the Big Hole River area with Drouillard, Lewis confirmed his thought as to which fork to take, *"I took the advantage of a high projecting spur of the mountain* (Lewis's Lookout) *which with some difficulty we ascended to it's summit in about half an hour. From this eminence I had a pleasing view of the valley through which I had passed many miles below and the continuation of the middle fork* (Beaverhead River) *through the valley... to the distance of about 20 miles...to enter the mountains...I did not hesitate in believing the middle fork the most proper for us to ascend."* Locals refer to this rocky ridge as the Hogback.

In their writings, Lewis and Clark called the entire length of the Jefferson and Beaverhead rivers *"Jefferson's River,"* but today's Jefferson begins where the Big Hole (*Wisdom*) and Beaverhead rivers mix their waters, north of Twin Bridges and downstream from the entrance of the Ruby (né *"Philanthropy"*) River. The Beaverhead originates further up at the joining of Red Rock River and Horse Prairie Creek.

You can follow this next segment of the Lewis and Clark Expedition route by driving south from Twin Bridges along the Beaverhead River on Hwy 41. About 12 miles from Twin Bridges you'll see Beaverhead Rock on your right. At Dillon, there is a diorama at the Chamber of Commerce on South Montana Street, depicting the departure of Lewis and his three men from the main party after Sacajawea had identified the Beaver's Head. From Dillon take I-15 south. Ten miles out, across from where the highway comes close to the east side of the river, are the Rattlesnake Cliffs. Then take the Clark Canyon exit. Head west across the dam and look for the Camp Fortunate Interpretive site. From there continue west on Road 324 through the Horse Prairie Valley, past the small community of Grant until a road sign points to Lemhi Pass. A very scenic dirt road leads to a pleasant picnic area and a tremendous view.

On their 104th day in what would become Montana and far behind the schedule they had envisioned for reaching the Pacific Ocean, the Corps struggled against the course of the present-day Beaverhead River. It was August 8, 1805, and from both sides of the waterway, a pleasant valley sprawled out, gradually rising to the numerous mountain ranges of the area. While the Ruby and Snowcrest climbed to the east, the Pioneers dominated the western horizon. Well to the south, the travelers could see the Tendoy and Blacktail mountains, all reminders of the demanding undertaking yet ahead of them.

The captains knew very soon their water route would end and they would have to cross the Rocky Mountains in order to reach the Columbia River and ultimately the Pacific Ocean. Several of the men were ill, others, including Captain Clark, had injuries, one man, Shannon, was lost, all were *"much fatigued from their excessive labours"* and as Lewis worried *"we have a stock already sufficiently small for the length of the voyage before us."* The morale of the Expedition team was at an all-time low. As summer was well along and signs of an early autumn beginning to appear, a sense of urgency existed to acquire horses from the Shoshone Indians. Clearly positive news was needed.

On the evening of August 8th, Lewis penned in his journal *"the Indian woman* (Sacajawea) *recognized the...hill she says her nation calls the beavers head from a conceived resemblance of its*

August 12, 1805, Lewis became the first known white man to cross the Continental Divide when he went through Lemhi Pass.
RICK AND SUSIE GRAETZ

figure to the head of that animal. she assures us that we shall either find her people on this river or on the river immediately west of its source..." Spirits and the journey's outlook took a rise!

Lewis, more determined now than ever to find the Shoshone Indians, even if it *"should cause me a trip of one month,"* made a decision to proceed ahead by land with three of his men. Clark and the others would rest and then continue by river.

Clark reiterated on August 9th, *"a fine morning...we proceeded on verry well...Shannon the man whome we lost on Wisdom River Joined us...game of every kind Scerce."*

Setting out early, Lewis and his group covered 16 miles spending the night near present-day Dillon, then on August 10th, they discovered an Indian trail reaching a series of 600-foot high crags the men dubbed *"rattle snake clifts"* for the copious number of *"serpents"* frequenting the place. Later, they passed a stream coming in from the west calling it *"Willard's Creek,"* which more than 50 years henceforth, would be known as Grasshopper Creek and live on as the gulch that spawned Montana's first major gold strike, thereby giving birth to Bannack, the original Montana Territorial Capital.

That afternoon, Lewis's group approached the confluence of Red Rock River and Horse Prairie Creek. Before construction of Clark Canyon Dam, the Beaverhead River was formed by these two flows, the junction of which is now under the reservoir's waters.

Once again the question. Which fork to follow? Leaving a note for Clark *"recommending it to him to halt at this place untill my return,"* Lewis pursued hoof prints leading up the Red Rock River until

Lewis — *"the Indian woman recognized... the hill she says her nation calls the beavers head."* North of Dillon.
RICK AND SUSIE GRAETZ

the markings disappeared in the dense brush. Retreating, he found different tracks headed west on Horse Prairie Creek that eventually led them to *"a beatifull and extensive plain...surrounded on all sides by a country of roling or high wavy plains through which several little rivulets extend their wide vallies quite to the Mountains which surround the whole in an apparent Circular manner; forming one of the handsomest coves I ever saw."* At this point, Lewis was describing Shoshone Cove or today's Horse Prairie Valley. He was looking at the Tendoys on the south and directly to the west, the Beaverhead Mountains, a segment of the Bitterroot Range that forms the Montana/Idaho border.

Shortly, Lewis observed through his spyglass, an Indian on horseback, who he assumed to be a Shoshone. Apparently alarmed, the Indian took off. Lewis was despaired that he had possibly lost all chances of obtaining horses. That night, they camped along Horse Prairie Creek.

The next morning, August 12th, the party followed a well-used route westward along a waterway now called Trail Creek upwards toward the Divide. The valley closed in as the footpath gradually climbed to the 7,373-foot high pass. Today's road probably approximates this Indian byway.

Lewis noted in his journal, *"...the road was still plain, I therefore did not dispair of shortly finding a passage over the mountains and of tasting the waters of the great Columbia this evening. At the distance of four miles further the road took us to the most distant fountain of the waters of the mighty Missouri in search of which we have spent so many toilsome days and wristless nights."* Actually, the most distant trickle of the Missouri comes from Hellroaring Creek, flowing out of the eastern end of the Centennial Mountains into the Red Rock River, a good distance to the east; not from the one Lewis thought.

Meriwether Lewis became the first known white man to cross the Continental Divide. *"we proceeded on to the top of the dividing ridge from which I discovered immence ranges of high mountains still to west with their tops partially covered with snow...I now descended the mountain about 3/4 of a mile which I found much steeper than on the opposite side...here I first tasted the water of the grat Columbia river."* Today this passage is called Lemhi Pass.

In order to explain the discrepancy in the movements of the two captains, it is interesting to note that while Lewis was moving fairly quickly cross-country and ascending mountain passes, Clark and his party were traveling 16–18 miles by water each day in order to gain a mere four miles by land. On the 13th of August, Clark stopped at *"McNeal's (Blacktail Deer) Creek after Hugh McNeal one of our party,"* and climbed a *"high Point of Limestone rocks,"* where he took compass readings to the course of the *"Wisdom river, Beaver head hill, gap at the place the river passes thro' a mountain (Rattlesnake Cliffs)."* Called Clark's Lookout, it is near the Dillon North I-15 interchange where State Route 41 crosses the river and intersects with I-15. This is one of only two places along the entire route where one can stand in the exact spot Clark did (the other is Pompey's Pillar, 30 miles east of Billings). They camped a few miles southwest of Dillon, where Clark wrote of the day, *"The river obliges the men to undergo great fatigue and labour in hauling the Canoes over the Sholes in the Cold water naked."*

And it was on that same August 13th, that one could say Lewis's prayers were answered. An Indian road, which *"appeared to have been much traveled lately both by men and horses,"* carried them *"down a long descending valley...to a large creek."* Leaving the creek bottom, they traveled through a wide depression in the hills when they *"were so fortunate as to meet with three female* savages," who were digging roots. Determined to introduce himself to the *"chiefs and warriors of their nation,"* Meriwether then *"bestoed an equivalent portion of trinkets...painted their tawny cheeks with some vermillion which with this nation is emblematic of peace. after they had become composed I informed them by signs that I wished them to conduct us to their camp...they readily obeyed and we set out, still pursuing the road down the river."*

A band of sixty well-armed Shoshone warriors on horseback charged the small group. Lewis laid down his rifle, and carrying only his flag, trailed behind the woman who exclaimed to the war party that these were gift-bearing whitemen. Welcomed in peace by Chief Cameahwait, Lewis and his men began their short stay at the Indian's main camp along the Lemhi River just north of today's Tendoy, Idaho.

Lacking guns to protect themselves from marauding tribes, the Shoshone were as Lewis wrote, *"obliged to live in the interiors of these mountains at least two thirds of the year where the suffered as we then saw great heardships for the want of food."* Though desperately poor and practically starving, the natives shared their meager supply of berries and roots with the white men. *"they live in a wretched stait of poverty...they are frank, communicative, fair in dealing, generous with the little they possess, extreemly honest, and by no means beggarly."*

Lewis, hoping to give Clark and the rest of his crew, who were having a long drawn-out and torturous struggle up the Beaverhead, enough time to arrive at the river junction, sought information. *"I now prevailed on the Chief to instruct me with rispect to the geography of this country...he drew the river on which we now are* (Lemhi River and on to the Salmon)*...he informed me...that there was no possibilyte of passing along the shore...and the rapidity of the stream such that the whole surface of the river was beat into perfect foam as far as the eye could reach. that the mountains were also inaccessible to man or horse."* This news was not good. Cameahwait then spoke of an arduous trail to the north used by the *"persed nose* (Nez Perce) *Indians...so thickly timbered that they could scarcely pass."* Lewis declared, *"my rout was instantly settled in my mind."*

Now, it was imperative for Lewis to unite with Clark and to eventually entice the Shoshone to trade for a quantity of horses sufficient enough to carry their supplies over the mountains. Convincing the chief and his people to accompany him back to his camp at the forks, they finally attained the rendezvous point on August 16th; and much to Lewis's dismay, Clark had yet to arrive. Then on the 17th, as the tardy crew came in sight of the campsite, Sacajawea, who was in front, immediately recognized her people and according to Clark, she *"danced for the joyful Sight."*

Once again, the Corps of Discovery's success hung in the balance. Favorable negotiations for horses and a guide to get them over the Nez Perce trail were requisite. An assembly was called and in "round robin" fashion, the serious and critical communications began. Chief Cameahwait spoke Shoshone to Sacajawea, who next translated the words into Hidatsa; Charbonneau in turn translated the thought into French; and Francis Labiche then conveyed the message in English to Lewis and Clark. During these convoluted conversations, Sacajawea *"in the person of Cameahwait...recognized her brother. She instantly jumped up, and ran and embraced him...weeping profusely."*

This was truly the Expedition's lucky day; appropriately, the leaders christened the meeting place "Camp Fortunate."

▸▸ The Beaverhead River, to the Corps this was the Jefferson... looking northeast towards the Tobacco Roots. CHUCK HANEY

Now, it was decided for Clark to head up and over Lemhi Pass, to discover whether or not the Salmon River was as impassable as the Indians had noted, while Lewis would remained at the campsite making pack saddles and constructing a cache of supplies to be used on the return trip. On August 26th, Clark informed Lewis by messenger, that the Salmon was indeed un-navigable. Upon hearing this, Lewis and his crew packed up and the two elements of the Expedition were reunited at the Indian village near Tendoy, Idaho. Lewis had crossed Lemhi pass three times, Clark only once; they never crossed it traveling together. It wasn't until 1855, when a group of Mormon settlers entered the valley and built Fort Lemhi, naming it for an ancient king who appears in the Book of Mormon that the pass got its name. Indians burned the fort two years later, but the name persisted.

The Bitterroot
River and
Como Peaks
of the Bitterroot
Mountains
south of
Hamilton.
RICK AND SUSIE GRAETZ

Through The Bitterroot To Lolo Pass

>>⟶

Horse traders they were not. August 30, 1805, the Corps of Discovery saddled up a band of mostly sorry looking, barely packable, sore-backed ponies and pulled out of the Shoshone camp. While it's true the impoverished and underfed Natives would need, and wanted to keep, their best horses for the impending buffalo hunt, it's hard to believe that with all of the trinkets and trading materials Lewis and Clark had, they couldn't have done a little better.

So off they rode with their native guide Old Toby, who knew the route to the Columbia. Following Idaho's Lemhi River to and up the North Fork of the present-day Salmon River, they gained the crest of the Bitterroot Mountains somewhere in the area of Lost Trail Pass. The date was September 3, 1805. Towards evening a wet snow began to make bushwhacking even harder, and poor visibility evidently hampered Old Toby's trail-blazing ability. In Clark's words, *"we passed over emence hils and Some of the worst roade that ever horses passed our horses frequently fell."*

Now we enter the phase that could be called by all of those trying to decipher the journals as the *"Where in the hell were they?"* part of the journey. There is a great deal of controversy among professional and amateur scholars alike as to the exact interpretation of Clark's notes. According to Stephen Ambrose in Undaunted Courage, *"The confusion of creeks and ravines cutting through the steep mountainsides has made the route the expedition used one of the most disputed of the entire journey,"* So suffice to say they may have stayed on the Divide for a while before dropping down on September 4th near the East Fork Bitterroot River and Sula at today's Ross's Hole.

Here they met the Salish who were on their way to the Three Forks to meet Cameahwait (Sacajawea's brother) and his Shoshone people to hunt buffalo. Clark estimated the encampment to be *"a nation of 33 Lodges about 80 men 400 Total and at least 500 horses."*

"these people received us friendly, threw white robes over our sholders & Smoked in the pipe of peace, we Encamped with them."

In the Discovering Lewis & Clark™ web site (www.lewis-clark.org), it is explained through stories handed down from Salish tribal elders, that to the Natives, the Corps was a very confusing sight. Because York was black skinned and warriors often painted themselves black when preparing for battle, perhaps they were the enemy. However, Sacajawea and her child were with them and this would have been unusual for a war party. With a wait and see attitude — besides the strangers were highly out numbered, the Salish deemed them to be friendly and welcomed them as was their custom.

Ridding themselves of some of the lesser desirable steeds, the Corps upgraded their herd by purchasing 11 *"ellegant horses"* and *"exchanged 7 for which we gave a fiew articles of merchendize."*

Leaving the Salish on September 6th, the men *"Crossed a Mountain (most likely Sula Peak),"* met and followed the East Fork Bitterroot River on the east side, camping a few miles northwest of Sula.

At first, the Captains called the present Bitterroot *"Flathead river"* and then soon thereafter renamed it *"Clarks river."*

Following the Bitterroot River north the next day, on a relatively easy course, the men had a close view of the seemingly insurmountable Bitterroot Range to the West, and as Sergeant Patrick Gass so aptly put it, *"the most terrible mountains I ever beheld."* Noticing snow on the mountains, they wondered if winter was making an early approach, and camped near today's Grantsdale on the east side of the river.

On September 8th, their night's stay was close to Stevensville on the right riverbank where numerous streams enter the Bitterroot.

Lewis's Journal entry of September 9, 1805 reads, *"Set out at 7 A M. this morning and proceeded down and the Flathead (Bitterroot) river leaving it on our left, the country in the valley of the this river is generally a prarie and from five to 6 miles wide,"* continuing downriver and eventually crossing to the west side *"encamped on a large creek (Lolo Creek) which falls in on the West as our guide informs us that we should leave the river at this place and the weather appearing settled and fair I determined to hault the next day to rest the horses and take some scelestial Observations. we called this Creek 'Travellers rest'."* The spot is located about one mile up from the creek's junction with the Bitterroot River by the town of Lolo. Now from Old Toby came the news of a much easier and shorter route beyond the Gates of the Mountains near Helena, probably over present-day Mullan Pass, up to Missoula and along the Clark Fork River to the Bitterroot. If they'd had horses, it would have taken the Corps a mere four days to reach this valley instead of an arduous 52-days.

About 1850, *"Travellers rest Creek"* became known as Lolo Creek. Local Indians had trouble with a French Canadian trapper's name. They couldn't pronounce the French uvular r, in Lawrence and shortened it to the easiest part…Lo-Lo, hence Lolo. And the onerous path the Corps was about to embark on, used for generations by Indians (principally the Nez Perce) on their way to hunt buffalo on the east side of the mountains, and said to be passable only with the knowledge of those who had been shown the way before, was first called the Nee Mee Poo (the Nez Perce's name for themselves) or Nez Perce Trail, then Lolo Trail. What ever it was called, it proved to be both tortuous and merciless.

John Colter of the Expedition, while out hunting on September 10th, met three Nez Perce Indians in search of a band of Shoshone horse thieves. They followed Colter back to camp, and conversing in sign language, one agreed to stay and guide them to his home on the Clearwater River, telling the captains the river was navigable and that *"it would require five sleeps wich is 6 days travel, to reach his relations."*

They also learned from these Indians of perhaps an even better route back to the Missouri. It involved following the Bitterroot River to the Clarks Fork then on to the Blackfoot and crossing an easy pass over the Divide (today's Lewis and Clark Pass) to the buffalo country near Augusta. The captains noted this route for their return. They had already heard of it from both the Hidatsas and the Shoshones, but never seemed to acknowledge it until now.

As the group was preparing to depart Travelers' Rest on September 11th, they discovered that two of their horses were missing and put off leaving to search for them. Consequently, the young Nez Perce who had offered to be their guide, grew impatient and left; but they still had Old Toby and traversed *"thro' a narrow valie and good road for 7 miles,"* camping a short ways north of Lolo Creek. Looking south, from this site, located on a private ranch, the imposing north faces of the two

Lewis and Clark
camped here on
Lolo Creek,
September 11,
1805, beneath
Lolo Peak.
RICK AND SUSIE GRAETZ

Travelers'
Rest at Lolo,
"home" from
September 9–11,
1805, before
crossing the
Bitterroots on
the way to the
Columbia River.
RICK AND SUSIE GRAETZ

Lolo Peaks are very visible. The route follows Hwy 12 and the approximate location of the camp is signed.

The mettle of the Corps was once again about to be tested. Clark's journal entry of September 12th describes, *"Set out at 7 oClock & proceeded on up the Creek...the road through this hilley Countrey is verry bad passing over hills & thro Steep hollows, over falling timber &c. &c. continued on & passed Some most intolerable road on the Sides of the Steep Stoney mountains...Crossed a mountain 8 miles with out water & and camped on a hill Side on the Creek after Decending a long Steep mountain...Party and horses much fatigued."* This camp at Spring Gulch, was approximately one mile below Lolo Hot Springs.

Friday the 13th lived up to its reputation. Had William Clark been superstitious, the day's calamities would have easily been attributed to it. *"Capt Lewis and one of our guides lost their horses...I proceeded on with the partey up the Creek at 2 miles past Several Springs which I observed...below one of the Indians had made a whole to bathe, I tasted this water and found it hot & not bad."* The natural springs have today been reduced to a swimming pool.

Noting that *"as Several roads led from these Springs in different derections, my guide took a wrong road and took us out of our rout 3 miles through intolerable rout, after falling into the right road I proceeded on thro tolerabl rout for abt. 4 or 5 miles and halted to let our horses graze as well as waite for Capt Lewis who has not yet Come up."*

Finally crossing the Montana/Idaho border on this the 13th of September 1805, tired, cold and miserable, the Expedition went down *"a Small (Pack) Creek"* to the beautiful Packer Meadows for the night.

They had gained the summit of the Bitterroot Range; and in passing out of Montana had a new adventure through Idaho, Washington and Oregon ahead of them before coming within sight of the Pacific Ocean on November 7, 1805. It took another month before the Corps selected the location for their winter camp. On December 7, 1805, they began construction of Fort Clatsop.

Trapper Peak, an imposing landmark in the Bitterroots.
JOHN LAMBING

The Bitterroot Valley served as the Expedition's "road" in early September 1805.
DONNY SEXTON/TRAVEL MONTANA

1806 — Return To Travelers' Rest

If the Corps of Discovery thought that the worst was behind them now that the Pacific Coast had been attained, they were in for a huge disappointment. The winter of 1805–1806 wasn't the most pleasant for the Explorers. Arriving at their chosen camp for the winter on December 7, 1805, the men were instructed to commence the building of the walled and gated structure that would be "home" for the next three and a half months. Dubbed Fort Clatsop after the local Indian tribe, it was located in northwest Oregon on the Lewis and Clark River southwest of today's Astoria. Of the 106 days they spent in this encampment, only 12 were without rain. The men were continually ill, no doubt largely due to their meager and boring diet and the cold, wet weather. It was an anxious band of men, who packed their measly belongings and supplies and on March 23, 1806, followed Lewis when he said, *"At 1P.M. we bid a final adieu to Fort Clatsop."*

Turning to the east back through Oregon, Washington and Idaho, the Expedition entered the west side of the Rocky Mountains in mid-June. Being unfamiliar with spring conditions at altitudes higher than the Adirondacks and other eastern mountains, Lewis and Clark were surprised when they encountered great amounts of snow. Clark described their frustration, *"on the 17th* (June 1806)...*the Snow became So deep in every direction from 6 to 8 feet deep we could not prosue the road...we were obliged to return to...precure meat to live on as well as grass for our horses...We precured 5 Indians as pilots and on the 24th of June 1806 we again under took those Snowey regn...on the 27th & 28th also passing over Snow 6 or 8 feet deep all the way."*

On June 29, 1806, the Corps with their five Nez Perce guides, crossing back into Big Sky Country, *"found the old road which we passed on as we went out...after dinner we continued our march 7 ms further to the worm Springs where we arrived early in the evening...Those Worm or Hot Springs are Situated at the base of a hill of no considerable hight, on the N. Side and near the bank of travellers rest (Lolo) Creek."* Camping here at the same spot Clark had passed and described on September 13, 1805, *"both the men and the indians amuse themselves with use of the bath this evening...after the Indians remaining in the hot bath as long as they could bear it run and plunge themselves into the Creek the water...Cold as ice Can make it; after remaining here a fiew minits they returned...repeating this transision several times but always ending with the warm bath."* Lewis and Clark joined the men in the wilderness hot tub, and became the first white customers of the future Lolo Hot Springs Resort.

Making good time moving down Lolo Creek on the 30th, Lewis and his horse met with a near tragic accident on a steep slope. He later related, *"I also met with the plant in blume which is sometimes called the lady's slipper or mockerson flower."* This was the rare mountain lady's slipper before unknown to science. Continuing down the trail, *"a little before Sunset we arrived at our old encampment on the S. Side of the Creek a little above its entrance into Clarks* (Bitterroot) *river and in here we Encamped with a view to remain 2 days in order to rest ourselves and horses and to make our final arrangements for Seperation."* The Corps of Discovery had returned to their previous Travelers' Rest camp of September 9, 10 and 11, 1805 just up Lolo Creek from the Hwy 93 bridge and Lolo.

Clark summed up the past two weeks of travel thusly, *"Descended the mountain to Travellers*

Lolo Creek along the old Nez Perce Trail that the Explorers followed on their trip to and from the Pacific.

RICK AND SUSIE GRAETZ

rest leaving those tremendious mountanes behind us — in passing of which we have experiensed Cold and hunger of which I shall ever remember."

Now the moment to execute the complex and timing sensitive plans for the major separation was at hand. It had been decided at their winter camp that Lewis would lead a party over land "as far as the Falls of Missouri," following a route the Nez Perce had mentioned the September past. There he would leave several men to build the equipment necessary for the portage. The rest of the crew would accompany him in exploring the Marias River hoping to prove that the northernmost sources of the Missouri River lay north of the 50th parallel, which would give the U.S. claim to more land (beaver territory).

Clark, in the mean time, would travel southeast to the cache at Camp Fortunate and then move down the Jefferson/Beaverhead River to Three Forks at which place several men from his group would paddle the canoes down the Missouri connecting with Lewis's construction party at the falls, *"and after passing the portage around the falls, proceed on down to the enterance of Maria where Captain Lewis will join them."* Clark's plan was to leave the Three Forks area, striking out eastward across the Gallatin Valley to reach the Yellowstone River and explore it to its confluence with the Missouri, where he and his men would reunite with Lewis and the rest of the Corps. It sounded good on paper, but for all of the separate groups to come together at the appropriate times would depend on a great deal of luck. One could perhaps liken the plan to the intricate maneuvers of a precision drill team; only in this instance, there would be no practice. They would have to get it right on the first try.

In order to keep confusion to a minimum, we will first follow Lewis's journey uninterrupted to the planned rendezvous with Clark at the confluence of the Yellowstone. Captain Clark will then get a turn to tell his portion of the story from Travelers' Rest in its entirety.

Lewis — A New Route To The Rendezvous

The separation date was July 3, 1806. Lewis, *"all arrangements being now completed...we saddled our horses and set out I took leave of my worthy friend and companion Capt. Clark and the party that accompanyed him. I could not avoid feeling much concern on this occasion although I hoped this seperation was only momentary. I proceeded...with my party of nine men and five Indians."*

Their route from Travelers' Rest took them down the Bitterroot River to just beyond the mixing of today's Bitterroot and Clark Fork rivers where they crossed. From there they traversed the Missoula Valley and camped at the mouth of Grant Creek. According to the Nez Perce, the path would continue along the Clark Fork to the Blackfoot River (*"Cokahlarishkit"* or *"the river of the road to the buffaloe."*) From there *"they informed us that not far from the dividing ridge* (Continental Divide) *between the waters of this and the Missouri rivers,"* the white men would have two choices, one would be a fork up and over Lewis and Clark Pass and the other to climb over Cadotte Pass. They recommended the Lewis and Clark gap as being closer and easier, *"and thence to medicine* (Sun) *river and the falls of the Missouri where we wished to go. they alledged that as the road was a well beaten track we could not now miss our way and as they were affraid of meeting their enimies the Minnetare* (Hidatsa) *they could not think of continuing with us any longer."*

Suddenly without guides, on July 4th Lewis rode east through the town of Missoula, along a path that approximates today's Broadway Street, previously Mullan Road, and then followed the Clark Fork past Rattlesnake Creek through Hell Gate Canyon, by Marshall Creek making a left turn onto the Blackfoot River. Their Independence Day 1806 camp was about eight miles up on the north side. Hwy 200 in part follows the Blackfoot River, but a segment of the river departs from the road and cuts its canyon to the north towards Ninemile Prairie. West of Clearwater Junction, the river comes closer to Hwy 200, or just south of it, and continues so as it meanders east past Lincoln to its headwaters. Lewis's progress on the "Indian Road" for the most part, stayed near the water.

July 5th they camped just up from where Monture Creek and the Blackfoot River join. To Lewis, Monture was *"Seamans' Creek"*, named for his Newfoundland dog. Lewis made note in his writings of the many *"knobs"* in this part of the valley. These hill-like features, a result of glaciation, are still visible today.

Lewis and his men made 25 miles the next day, passing the North Fork of the Blackfoot east of Ovando and cutting across the north end of Nevada Valley near Helmville that Hwy 200 intersects. A *"crooked pond"* he mentions is probably Kleinschmidt or Browns lake. All day long, they had seen both fresh and old signs of what they thought were the *"Minnetares of Fort de prarie."* Camp for the night of July 6th was on Beaver Creek, which flows into the Blackfoot from the north about two miles west of Lincoln.

In the morning, they kept on a course along *"a level beautiful plain on the north side of"* the Blackfoot River, and then in the vicinity of Keep Cool Creek and Landers Fork, left the Blackfoot Valley and ascended several ridges to Alice Creek. Alice Creek and Landers Fork are two of the main flows that start the Blackfoot River on its westward course.

Missoula, Lewis's trail to the Blackfoot took him along Broadway St. and through Hell Gate Canyon.
LARRY MAYER

Blackfoot River
west of Lincoln.
RICK AND SUSIE GRAETZ

Near Monture
Creek — the
"Knobs" Lewis
described in the
Blackfoot Valley.
RICK AND SUSIE GRAETZ

Alice Creek, which heads along the Continental Divide, pushes through a narrow canyon before meandering down its *"handsome narrow plain."* Lewis had no trouble following the well-marked route to today's Lewis and Clark Pass (named such although Clark never set foot on it). A dirt road follows Alice Creek and just before the river corridor narrows, a Forest Service sign notes Lewis's as well as the Indians' path through this country. The road ends in what is now Alice Creek Basin and an old road (now a trail) climbs to the pass. It's an easy trek of about two miles. Faint signs of the travois tracks of countless thousands of Indians who crossed here on their way to and from the bison hunting grounds are still visible.

Indications are that the Hidatsa near Fort Mandan had mentioned this route and that the Corps missed it on their way west. Jefferson's instructions were to follow the Missouri. The question is whether he meant for them to trace it to its headwaters or if it was more important to find the most direct route to the Pacific Ocean. According to popular opinion at the time and the Nicholas King map the two captains carried with them, the headwaters of the Columbia and Missouri rivers would connect near the 45th parallel making for a relatively easy portage over the top of the Divide. Naturally, if one believed this to be true — and it seemed that not only Lewis and Clark, but also the President did, then following the Missouri to its headwaters "would" be the most direct route to the Pacific Ocean. But all conjecture about "short cuts" still comes down to the fact, they needed the horses to cross the Rocky Mountains and for that, they had to meet the Shoshone.

From the height of the pass, Lewis described seeing *"fort mountain* (Square Butte),*"* a landmark they named the previous summer. Only the north end is visible from this point as other prairie landforms block much of it. They camped about three miles to the east of Table Mountain (a Rocky Mountain Front peak) near Cuniff Basin, south of Bean Lake. This area can be viewed from State Road 435, a dirt byway that points north of Hwy 200 from west of Bowmans Corners and stretches along the Rocky Mountain Front to Augusta.

At 6:00 in the morning on July 8th, the party broke camp, topped a hill and set eyes on what they called *"Shishequaw mountain* (the very distinctive and easily identified Haystack Butte)*...a high insulated conic mountain standing several miles in advance of the Eastern range of the rocky mountains."* Three miles later, they passed the upper reaches of *"Dearborne's river."* It was just 10 days short of a year since they had named it on the trip west. Lewis and his men had once again arrived at the immense open expanse of prairie that gives Montana its "Land of the Big Sky" name. The men are *"much rejoiced at finding ourselves in the plains of the Missouri which abound with game."*

The party was heading northeast towards the Sun River at a point about three to four miles west of Augusta. From here they would track the Sun to the Missouri. Highways 21 and 200 go through the Valley of the Sun for a portion of the course that Lewis followed. Camp that night was about 14 miles east of Augusta on an island in the Sun River just north of Hwy 21 where the captain *"killed a very large and the whitest woolf I have seen."*

On July 9th, they covered a mere eight miles, because of the cold, rainy weather; they camped on the south side of the Sun River about one mile northwest of the town of Simms near Simms Creek.

Bear, *"several gangs of elk, vast assemblages of wolves,"* deer, *"vast herds of buffalo"* and *"gooseberries are very abundant."* The food bank was looking better all the time. July 10, 1806 after traversing *"beautiful level and smooth...high praries and plains,"* they stopped for the night *"in a grove of cottonwood timber"* on the banks of the Sun River about four miles west of the edge of present-day Great Falls.

Lewis, July 11th, *"the morning was fair...the air was pleasant and a vast assemblage of little birds which croud to the groves on the river sung most enchantingly...proceeded with the party across the plain to the white bear islands which I found to be 8 ms. distant...through a level beautifull and extensive high plain covered with immence hirds of buffaloe...when I arrived in sight of the whitebear Islands the missouri bottoms on both sides of the river were crouded with buffaloe. I sincerely belief that there were not less than 10 thousand buffaloe within a circle of two miles around that place."* He encamped for the night on the west bank of the Missouri across from the White Bear Islands just below the mouth of Sand Coulee Creek, intending to give *"my horses a couple of days rest."*

On July 12th, according to Lewis, *"ten of our best horses were absent and not to be found. I fear they are stolen. I dispatched two men on horseback in surch of them."* Only three were found. That night *"we swam our horses over"* to the east side of the river just below the islands and *"encamped at sunset."*

It had been one year since they had cached supplies and specimens they hoped to bring to Washington DC, and experienced the very difficult portage and the disappointment of the iron boat. Upon opening the cache on July 13th, it was discovered that seepage from high spring water had ruined the entire collection of the carefully preserved plant specimens. Luckily, equipment needed for the portage was still usable as was the map.

In uncovering the carriage wheels on the 14th, Lewis *"found them in good order."* Also, *"the iron frame of the boat had not suffered materially."* Since there is no mention of salvaging the iron boat and carrying it with them on the 1806 return trip, speculation has it that the frame is still buried somewhere in the area and high-tech methods are being used in the search.

By the 15th, with only ten horses left, Lewis cut the Marias exploration party from the planned seven to four men — himself, the two Field brothers Reubin and Joseph, and the competent frontiersman and interpreter Drouillard. They would take six of the horses leaving *"two of the best and two of the worst...to assist the party in taking the canoes and baggage over the portage."*

The provisions were ready, and on July 16, 1806, using a *"canoe of buffaloe skins"* (they had made two) to ferry the baggage, Lewis and the three men *"were compelled to swim the horses above the whitebear island and again across medicine (Sun) river as the Missouri is of great width below the mouth of that river. having arrived safely below Medicine river we immediatly sadled our horses and proceeded down the river to the handsom fall (Rainbow Falls) of 47 feet where I halted about 2 hours and took a haisty sketch of these falls...after which we proceeded to the grand falls where we arrived at sunset...here we encamped...we see a number of goats or antilopes...they appear very inquisitive usually to learn what we are as we pass, and frequently accompany us at no great distance for miles...they are a very pretty animal and astonishingly fleet and active.*

In leaving the falls the next day, Lewis would head more or less in a northerly direction, through an area known today as the "Golden Triangle" for its extensive high-yield wheat fields. His mission was to establish the northernmost point of the Louisiana Purchase. If the Marias River was navi-

gable into Canada, a trade route up it would enable Americans to compete with the British in the fur trade business across the border. Over the next two days, proceeding to the west of Floweree, Carter, Fort Benton and Loma, and passing through Antelope Flats, their goal was to arrive at the Marias near the furthest most point he had explored the year before.

July 17th, *"...we took breakfast and departed. it being my design to strike Maria's river about the place at which I left it on my return to it's mouth in the begining of June 1805. I steered my course through the wide and level plains which have somewhat the appearance of an ocean, not a tree nor a shrub to be seen."* Their camp that evening was ten miles or so north and west of Carter.

July 18th, *"...ascended the river hills and continued our rout as yesterday through the open plains at about 6 miles we reached the top of an elivated plain which divides the waters of the rose* (Teton) *river from those of Maria's river. from hence the North mountains* (Bears Paw Mountains), *the South mountains* (Highwoods), *the falls mountains* (most likely the Little Belts) *and the Tower Mountain and those arround and to the East of the latter* (the Sweetgrass Hills) *were visible."* Each of these island ranges, owing to their substantial relief above the surrounding prairie, has a widespread presence from distances up to 100 miles away.

"...after dinner we proceeded about 5 miles across the plain to Maria's river where we arrived at 6 P. M...encamped on it's west side in a grove of cottonwood some miles above the entrance of the creek (Dugout Coulee, about three miles west of where Hwy 223 between Fort Benton and Chester crosses the Marias). *being now convinced that we were above the point to which I had formerly*

△ Alice Creek Valley,
west of the Continen-
tal Divide.
RICK AND SUSIE GRAETZ

▷ Lewis and Clark Pass,
crossed July 7, 1806.
RICK AND SUSIE GRAETZ

▷▷ Haystack Butte along
the Rocky Mountain
Front southeast of
Augusta.
DOUGLASS DYE

East of the
mountains,
bison supplied
the Corps with
skins and
sustenance.
RICK AND SUSIE GRAETZ

90

ascended this river." Constantly aware of the possible dangers associated with meeting the *"Minnetares of Fort de prarie and the blackfoot Indians...as they are a vicious lawless...set of wretches."* Lewis noted, *"I keep a strict lookout every night, I take my tour of watch with the men."*

July 19th, *"...the broken 'Mountains' so called from their raggid and irregular shape there are three of them extending from east to West almost unconnected, the center mountain terminates in a conic spire and is that which I have called the tower mountain they are destitute of timber."* The Sweetgrass Hills were being described; they consist of three distinct buttes or mountains...West Butte, Gold Butte or *"Tower Mountain"* and East Butte. Covering 20 miles and now heading decidedly west, they passed the then non-existent Tiber Dam and bedded down on the north shore of today's Lake Elwell, a mile or so on the west side of the Toole County/Liberty County line.

July 20th, *"...proceed through the open plain as yesterday up the North side of the river. the plains are more broken...and have become more inferior in point of soil; a great quanty of small gravel is every where distributed over the surface of the earth which renders travling extreemly painfull to our bearfoot horses...the mineral salts* (saline seep) *common to the plains of the missouri has been more abundant today than usual. The bluffs of the river are about 200 feet high."* That night, they camped just west of where I-15 crosses the Marias south of Shelby.

July 21st, numerous steep ravines, caused them to pass from the north side of the river to the south side and then back to the north before they *"took our course through the plains...at 2 P. M. we struck a northern branch of Marias river* (Cut Bank Creek)*...being convinced that this stream came from the mountains I determined to pursue it as it will lead me to the most nothern point to which the waters of Maria's river extend which I now fear will not be as far north as I wished and expected."* Cut Bank Creek merges here with the Two Medicine River to form the Marias River, as we know it today. Traveling north once again, they set camp just below the town of Cut Bank on the west side of the creek.

July 22nd, *"...for the first seven miles of our travel this morning the country was broken...the river* (Cut Bank Creek) *is confined closely between clifts of perpendicular rocks in most parts...we continued up the river on it's South side for 17 miles...we passed the river and took our course through a level and beaitifull plain on the N. side...the country has now become level, the river bottoms wide and the adjoining plains but little elivated above them...we had traveled 12 miles further when we arrived at a clump of large cottonwood trees in a beautifull and extensive bottom of the river about 10 miles below the foot of the rocky mountains where this river enters them; as I could see from hence very distinctly where the river entered the mountains and the bearing of this point being S of West I thought it unnecessary to proceed further and therefore encamped resolving to rest ourselves and horses a couple of days at this place...this plain on which we are is very high; the rocky mountains to the S. W. of us appear but low from their base up yet are partially covered with snow nearly to their bases...I now have lost all hope of the waters of this river ever extending to N Latitude 50."* Another great letdown for Lewis; and so, fittingly, he later names the spot *"Camp Disappointment."*

The explorers were looking at the snowy peaks of Glacier National Park to the west. The approximate site of their camp is reached by a going west on U.S. Hwy 2 from Cut Bank towards Browning. A right turn on MT 444 (Meriwether Road) towards the Port of Bonita leads to a well-marked turn off on the left side of the highway near Cut Bank Creek. The site is privately owned and tours to it from the Camp Disappointment Campground are available for a small fee.

The next three days were spent resting and attempting to obtain *"the necessary data to establish it's longitude"* and hunting. Only the first objective was successful. The cloudy weather hid the moon and the sun making celestial observations impossible and the men found game to be scarce.

The proverbial clock was ticking. *"I now begin to be apprehensive that I shall not reach the United States within this season unless I make every exertion in my power which I shall certainly not omit when once I leave this place."* And so on July 26th, *"we set out biding a lasting adieu to this place...I took my rout through the open plains SE...struck a principal branch of Maria's river (Two Medicine River)...not very deep, I passed this stream to it's south side and continued down it...when another branch (Badger Creek) formed a junction with it."*

Lewis's strategy was to follow the Two Medicine River to its joining with Cut Bank Creek and then go cross country to the Teton River, and from it to the Marias at Loma, there to meet up with the men and canoes from the portage. By staying off-river, he hoped to avoid contact with the Indians he assumed were hunting buffalo along the upper Marias.

After lunch, Lewis and the Field brothers rode up out of the river bottom to continue on the prairie, while Drouillard (or *"Drewyer"* as Lewis incorrectly referred to him) stayed alongside the stream. Lewis was about to the summit of the hill, when he noted several Indians with nearly 30 horses intently watching Drouillard. Now, uttering the biggest understatement of the entire journey — *"this was a very unpleasant sight,"* he assessed the situation, and feeling he had no choice but to approach the Indians in a friendly manner, did so.

The eight Indians were Piegans, a branch of the much-feared Blackfeet Nation. The captain gave the three "chiefs" gifts, and *"as it was growing late in the evening I proposed that we should remove to the nearest part of the river and encamp together...we descended a very steep bluff about 250 feet high to the river where there was a small bottom of nearly ½ mile in length."*

There is controversy concerning the precise locale of the "fight site" as it is called. Several Lewis and Clark scholars have a difference of opinion on the subject. Gary Moulton, in volume 8 of his The Journals of the Lewis and Clark Expedition, admirably explains: *"The limitations of Lewis's journal comments, course and distance references, and compass sightings, along with the similarity of terrain in the area opens the possibility that other nearby spots may be likely competitors for the designation. Due to the difficulties involved, an incontestable locating of the site may never be made. The same can be said for pinpointing most of Lewis and Clark camps."*

All seem to be going well. Then in the early morning hours of July 27th, while Joseph Fields was on guard duty, the eight warriors stole the guns from Lewis and his men, and in the ensuing fight to wrestled the weapons back, *"R Fields as he seized his gun stabed the indian to the heart with his knife the fellow ran about 15 steps and fell dead."* Lewis, Drouillard and Joseph Fields also successfully recovered their weapons, and *"as soon as they found us all in possession of our arms they ran and I now hollowed to the men and told them to fire on them if they attempted to drive off our horses, they accordingly pursued the main party who were drving the horses up the river and I pursued the man who... was driving off a part of the horses which were to the left of the camp...I called to them... that I would shoot them if they did not give me my horse and raised my gun, one of*

Rainbow,
one of the five
falls Lewis
discovered.
RICK AND SUSIE GRAETZ

The Sun, or
*"Medicine
River"* east of
Augusta.
RICK AND SUSIE GRAETZ

*them…turned arround and stoped at the distance of 30 steps from me and I shot him through the belly, he fell to his knees…and fired…he overshot me, being bearheaded I felt the wind of his bullet very distinctly. not having my shotpouch I could not reload my piece…I therefore returned leasurely towards camp, on my way I met with Drewyer…I desired him to haisten to the camp with me and assist in catching as many of the indian horses as were necessary…we had caught and saddled the horses and began to arrange the packs when the Fieldses returned with four of our horses; we left one of our horses and took four of the best of those of the indian's…we took some of their buffaloe meat and set out ascending the bluffs by the same rout we had decended last…my design was to hasten to the entrance of Maria's river as quick as possible in the hope of meeting with the canoes and party at that place having no doubt but that they would pursue us with a large party…no time was therefore to be lost and we pushed our horses as hard as they would bear. at 8 miles we passed a large branch…I called battle river (Birch Creek)"…*later, they skirted the town of Conrad. *"at 3 P. M. we arrived at rose river (Teton) about 5 miles above where we had passed it as we went out, having traveled by my estimate…about 63 ms. here we halted an hour and a half took some refreshment and suffered our horses to graize…after dinner…we again ascended the hills on the S. W. side and took the open plains; by dark we had traveled about 17 miles further, we now halted to rest ourselves and horses about 2 hours…after refreshing ourselves we again set out by moon light…we traveled untill 2 OCk in the morning having come by my estimate after dark about 20 ms. we now turned out our horses and laid ourselves down to rest in the plain very much fatiegued as may be readily conceived (they were about 16 miles west of Fort Benton). my indian horse carried me very well in short much better than my own would have done and leaves me with but little reason to complain of the robery."*

July 28th, *"I awaked the men and directed the horses to be saddled, I was so soar from my ride yesterday that I could scarcely stand, and the men complained of being in a similar situation…we again resumed our march…we had proceeded about 12 miles on an East course when we found ourselves near the Missouri; we heared a report which we took to be that of a gun but were not certain; still continuing down the N.E. bank of the Missouri about 8 miles further, being then within five miles of the grog spring (named the year before) we heard the report of several rifles…we quickly repared to this joyfull sound and on arriving at the bank of the river had the unspeakable satisfaction to see our canoes coming down."*

The puzzle was coming together; three of the fragmented troops were now reunited. Sergeant Ordway and his crew of nine men who had left Clark at Three Forks to bring canoes down the Missouri had caught up with Sergeant Gass and the five men Lewis left behind at the Lower Portage Camp. Now joined with the four Marias explorers, the party of 20 headed out to open the caches established at *"Decision Point"* the previous year. Finding some damage to the materials, they salvaged all they could and then freed the horses. Since the red pirogue was too decayed to be of use, they set off down the Missouri aboard the white pirogue and five smaller canoes; finally after 15 miles, stopping for the night just past the mouth of Crow Coulee.

During the spring of 1805, moving against the flow, it had taken the Corps approximately 37 days to cover the distance from the confluence of the Yellowstone River to the Marias; this time Lewis's contingent, going with the current, consumed only 11 days. As he passed by them, Lewis

▶▶ The Marias
south of
Shelby, Lewis
camped near
here on July 20,
1806.
CHUCK HANEY

Cut Bank Creek by
"Camp Disappointment"
July 22–26, 1806.
RICK AND SUSIE GRAETZ

Near the *"fight site"* of
Lewis's clash with eight
Blackfeet on July 27, 1806.
RICK AND SUSIE GRAETZ

The Missouri threads
through the western area
of the CMR National
Wildlife Refuge.
LARRY MAYER

again made mention in his Journals of some of the landforms and rivers he had discussed a year earlier.

July 29th, *"...we set out early and the currant being strong we proceeded with great rapidity...at 11 A. M. we passed that very interesting part of the Missouri where the natural walls appear* (White Cliffs section of the Upper Missouri River Breaks National Monument)*...encamped on the N. E. side of the river at the same place we had encamped on the 29th of May 1805* (near Slaughter Creek)*...the river is now nearly as high as it has been this season and is so thick with mud and sand that it is with difficulty I can drink it. every little rivulet now discharges a torrant of water bringing down immece boddies of mud sand and filth from the plains and broken bluffs."* This is an unusual condition for late July on the Missouri in north central Montana. From the reports in the Journals the prairie was experiencing an extremely wet summer.

July 30th, *"...the currant being strong and the men anxious to get on they plyed their oars faithfully and we went at the rate of about seven miles an hour...the rain continued with but little intermission all day."* They camped that night below Cow Creek.

July 31st, *"The rain still continuing...late in the evening we took sheter in some Indian lodges built of sticks."* This camp was somewhere below Rock Creek.

August 1st, *"The rain still continuing...I halted at this place about 15 ms. below Mussel shell river."* The party remained here drying the baggage and themselves out until the morning of the 3rd, *"we are all extremely anxious to reach the entrance of the Yellowstone river where we expect to join Capt. Clark and party."*

By Culbertson, the Missouri nears its meeting with the Yellowstone.
LARRY MAYER

August 4th, "...passed the entrance of big dry river; found the water in this river about 60 yds. wide tho' shallow (it had been dry when they passed in the spring of 1805)...at 3 P. M. we arrived at the entrance of Milk river where we halted a few minutes. this stream is full at present and it's water is much the colour of that of the Missouri...we encamped this evening two miles below the gulph on the N. E. side of the river." This camp was just before the location of their May 7, 1805 camp.

August 5th, "...we continued our rout until late in the evening...and encamped on the South side about 10 miles below little dry river (Prairie Elk Creek)." This was around four miles before Wolf Point. That night, "A little after dark...a violent storm arrose to the N. E. and shortly after came on attended with violent Thunder lightning and some hail; the rain fell in a mere torrant and the wind blew so violently that it was with difficulty I could have the small canoes unloaded before they filled with water."

August 6th, camp that evening was past the town of Poplar below Mortarstone Bluff near Brockton.

August 7th, "...we set out early resolving if possible to reach the Yelowstone river today which was at the distance of 83 ms. from our encampment of the last evening...we passed the entrance of Marthy's river (Big Muddy Creek) which has changed it's entrance since we passed it last year...at 4 P. M. we arrived at the entrance of the Yellowstone river. I landed at the point and found that Capt. Clark had been encamped at this place and from appearances had left it about 7 or 8 days. I found a paper on a pole at the point which mearly contained my name in the hand wrighting of Capt. C. we also found the remnant of a note which had been attatched to a peace of Elk's horns in the camp; from this fragment I learned that game was scarce at the point and musquetoes troublesome which were the reasons given for his going on." Clark actually left the note for Lewis on August 4th. They had missed the intended rendezvous by a mere three days, an astounding feat considering all the unknown country they'd all had to negotiate.

On the 12th of August in present day North Dakota Lewis met Clark. The Corps of Discovery was whole again.

Besides being a source
of nutrition for the
Corps, elk supplied
skins for clothing
and *"mockersons."*
RICK AND SUSIE GRAETZ

Sandstone rock
formations along
the Missourri.
RICK AND SUSIE GRAETZ

From Tripp Divide
looking towards the
Missouri and the
eastern edge of UL
Bend, the camp of
May 19, 1805 was
on the far side of the
river near here.
RICK AND SUSIE GRAETZ

102

The Big Hole
or *"Wisdom
River"* along
Clark's route in
early July 1806.
RICK AND SUSIE GRAETZ

Clark — On To The Yellowstone

Dressed in its finest, the Bitterroot Valley was preparing to face summer. The array of colorful wildflowers blending with the new mint green of the cottonwoods and aspens was offset by the glistening white of the snow-covered Bitterroot Range that flanks the valley to the west. Amidst this splendor, Clark traveled to the headwaters of the Bitterroot River. His trail passed familiar sights from the previous September and led to a crossing of the Continental Divide near Gibbons Pass, to the north of Lost Trail and Chief Joseph passes. He then rode through the Big Hole Valley and on to their Camp Fortunate of August 1805. Carrying out his segment of the plan developed during the winter at Fort Clatsop, Clark's mission was to explore the Yellowstone River to see if it was navigable and to encourage development of trade with the Indian tribes.

July 3, 1806, *"we colected our horses and after brackfast I took My leave of Capt Lewis and the Indians with (19) men interpreter Shabono & his wife & child...we proceeded on through the Vally of Clarks (Bitterroot) river on the West Side...This evening we Crossed 10 Streams 8 of which were large Creeks which Comes roleing their Currents with Velocity into the river. those Creeks Take their rise in the mountains to the West (Bitterroot Range) which mountains is at this time covered with Snow...Some snow is to be Seen on the high points and hollows of the mountains to the East of us (Sapphire Range)...we encamped on the north side of a large creek* (Blodgett Creek north a few miles from Hamilton)." What a difference Clark would see today. U.S. Hwy 93 imitates his valley route past farms and the towns of Stevensville and Victor.

Even after all of this time in the wilderness, Captain Clark was as patriotic as ever and couldn't forget the 4th of July. *"This being the day of the decleration of Independence of the United States and a Day commonly Scelebrated by my Country I had every disposition to Selebrate this day and therefore halted early and partook of a Sumptious Dinner of a fat Saddle of venison and Mush of Cows."* With that done, it was back on the trail, fording the numerous creeks coming out of the Bitterroots. After first passing by Hamilton and then later Darby, their camp that night was close to the confluence of the West and East forks of the Bitterroot above Connor.

The rivers and creeks in the area had been running fast and high with snowmelt making crossings dangerous and soaking their provisions. On July 5th, as they turned to follow the East Fork of the Bitterroot, Clark stopped opposite the mouth of Warm Springs Creek *"to let our horses graze and dry our wet articles...which detained us until ½ past 4 P. M. we packed up and Crossed the Mountain (by Sula),"* and came upon an Indian road used by the *"Oat lash shoots"* or Salish, that *"will evidently Shorten our rout at least 2 days...if I can prosue it my rout will be nearer and much better than the one we Came from the Shoshones, & if I should not be able to follow their road; our rout can't possibly be much wors."* This night was spent on Camp Creek near today's Camp Creek Ranger Station and U.S. Hwy 93.

Leaving the East Fork of the Bitterroot River, the party followed Camp Creek and their route of the previous September for three miles, then leaving the familiar path, veered in favor of the Salish road and *"assended a ridge with a gentle Slope to the dividing mountain (Continental Divide)."*

Crossing in the vicinity of Gibbons Pass, the men went down *"Glade (*Trail) *Creek"* along Hwy 43 and dropped into the Big Hole Valley. Here *"the Indian woman wife to Shabono informed me that she had been in this plain frequently and knew it well that the Creek which we decended was a branch of Wisdom river and when we assended the higher part of the plain we would discover a gap in the mountains* (Big Hole Pass) *in our direction to the Canoes* (Camp Fortunate) *and when we arived at that gap we would See a high point of a mountain* (Tendoy Mountains that flank the southern edge of Horse Prairie Valley) *covered with snow in our direction to the canoes."* The group ended up the night of July 6th, near Moose Creek about seven miles southwest of the small community of Wisdom, named after the Corps of Discovery's *"Wisdom River"* now the Big Hole River.

Leaving the Wisdom area on July 7th, Clark and his men turned south and *"proceeded on through an open rich vally...Sometimes following an old road which frequently disappeared, at the distance of 16 miles we arived at a Boiling Spring* (Jackson Hot Springs)...*it has every appearance of boiling, too hot for a man to endure his hand in it 3 seconds. I directt Sergt. Pryor and John Shields to put each a peice of meat in the water of different Sises. the one about the Size Of my 3 fingers Cooked dun in 25 minits the other much thicker was 32 minits before it became Sufficiently dun."* Too scorching to bathe in then, the springs are a favorite destination for today's travelers. Continuing on, they crossed over Big Hole Pass to *"some butifull Springs which fall into Willards* (Grasshopper) *Creek,"* camping in the vicinity of the headwaters of Divide Creek.

In tribute to the bounty of the landscape they had passed through, Clark wrote, *"This extensive vally Surround with mountains* (the Bitterroot Range and West Pioneer)...*covered with snow is extreemly fertile...and the Creeks which pass through it contains emence numbers of beaver &c. I now take my leave of this butifull extensive vally which I call the hot spring Vally, and behold one less extensive and much more rugid on Willards Creek."* In the latter part, Clark was referring to the land to the east of the ghost town/State Park of Bannack and south to Horse Prairie Creek.

The route through this area on U.S. Hwy 93 south from Lolo towards Chief Joseph Pass and then Hwy 43 to the Big Hole Valley where Road 278, from Wisdom through Jackson, over and down Big Hole Pass to the gravel road leading to Bannack and the Horse Prairie Creek Valley, somewhat approximates their trail.

On the 8th of July, following an Indian road down Divide Creek, they turned and traveled across the valley to Horse Prairie Creek where *"we proceeded on down the forke...9 Miles to our encampment of 17 Augt.* (1805, Camp Fortunate) *at which place we* (had) *Sunk our Canoes & buried Some articles...most of the Party with me being Chewers of Tobacco become So impatient to be chewing it that they Scercely gave themselves time to take their Saddles off their horses before they were off to the deposit. I found every article Safe, except a little danip. I gave to each man who used tobacco about two feet off a part of a role took one third of the ballance myself...as it was late nothing Could be done with the Canoes this evening. I examined them and found then all Safe except one of the largest which had a large hole in one Side & Split in bow."* In summing up their segment of the return journey so far, Clark noted, *"The road which we have traveled from travellers rest Creek to this place...with only a few trees being cut out of the way would be an excellent waggon road...one Mountain of about 4 miles over excepted which would require a little digging...The distance is 164 miles."* The day of the 9th was spent drying out and repairing the canoes for the next day's departure.

Sunrise over
the Sapphire
Mountains and
the Bitterroot
Valley.
RICK AND SUSIE GRAETZ

In the Bitterroot
Valley.
RICK AND SUSIE GRAETZ

Confluence of the
Madison and Jefferson
rivers just above the
mouth of the Gallatin.
JOHN LAMBING

Clark crossed Big Hole
Pass on July 7, 1806,
and took his leave "*of
this butifull extensive
vally.*"
RICK AND SUSIE GRAETZ

The Tendoy Mountains
and Horse Prairie Creek
Valley. Clark passed
near here on his way
to Camp Fortunate.
RICK AND SUSIE GRAETZ

On July 10, 1806, with Sergeant Pryor, Captain Clark and six men on horseback, and Sergeant Ordway in charge of the canoes, *"all Set out at the Same time & proceeded on Down jeffersons (Beaverhead) river...through Sarviss Vally and rattle snake mountain* (Rattlesnake Cliffs just south of Dillon) *and into that butifull and extensive Vally open and fertile which we Call the beaver head Vally...this Vally extends from the rattle Snake Mountain down jeffersons river as low as fraziers Creek* (South Boulder River). At mid-day, after making 15 miles, Clark halted the horses to let them graze and ordered the canoes to land. Sergeant Ordway informed him *"he thought the Canoes could go as farst as the horses &c. as the river now become wider and not So Sholl."* Upon hearing this, Captain Clark chose to desert the cavalry and join the Navy. He then *"directed Sergt. Pryor to proceed on moderately and if possible encamp with us every night...Set out, and proceeded on tolerable well to the head of the 3000 Mile Island...opposite this island I encamped on the East side."*

At this time, they were already ten miles north of Dillon. In one day, the canoes and horses had easily covered the same distance it had previously taken the adventurers six days on their westward trek. Though the voyage was far from effortless and mishaps not uncommon, one has to think at some point, recalling their incredibly torturous struggle going up the river a year ago, they sat back and said, "Now, this is the way to travel!"

This "southern contingent" of the Expedition continued following the river passing familiar scenes and landmarks, and on July 11th, they camped about two miles north of Twin Bridges at the mouth of the Big Hole River. They would now be following the Jefferson River and on the 12th, camped several miles east of the Lewis and Clark Caverns and about two miles below the mouth of Antelope Creek. Hwy 287 crosses the river near here.

On July 13th, Clark penned, *"proceded on very well to the enterance of Madicines river at our old Encampment of the 27th July last* (they were back at the Three Forks of the Missouri) *at 12 where I found Sergt. Pryor and party with the horses."* Their previous upstream trip took 21 days, this downstream one just three and a half.

Losing no time, they *"had all the baggage of the land party taken out of the Canoes and after dinner the 6 Canoes and the party of 10 men under the direction of Sergt. Ordway Set out. previous to their departur I gave instructions how they were to proceed &c. I also wrote to Capt Lewis."* Sergeant Ordway and his men's destination was the Great Falls on the Missouri where they were to join Sergeant Gass's party, portage around the falls and meet Captain Lewis at the mouth of the Marias.

Now, the Corps was fragmented into three separate units. When Lewis and his men leave the Great Falls party to explore the Marias on the 16th of July, and when it is time for Sergeant Pryor's group to take the horses overland to the Mandans, five small bands of men, each with its own mission, will forge ahead, all hoping to safely reunite in a relatively short period of time.

Included in Clark's crew going to the Yellowstone, were nine men, the Charbonneau family and 50 horses. *"at 5. P. M. I Set out from the head of Missouri at the 3 forks, and proceeded on nearly East 4 miles and Encamped on the bank of Gallitines River which is a butifull navigable Stream...The Country in the forks between Gallitins & Madisens rivers is a butifull leavel plain* (Gallatin Valley) *Covered with low grass on the lower or N E. Side of Gallitins river the Country rises gradually to the foot of a mountain* (Bridger Range) *which runs nearly parrelal...I observe Several leading roads*

which appear to pass to a gap of the mountain in a E. N E. direction about 18 or 20 miles distant. (Clark is looking to the north end of the Bridgers and probably can see Flathead Pass, an opening that crosses over to the Shields Valley)...*The indian woman who has been of great Service to me as a pilot through this Country recommends a gap in the mountain more South* (Bozeman Pass) *which I shall cross."* The young mother, who the captains frequently relied on for information, proved to be more valuable to the Expedition than her husband.

 Camp for the night of July 13th was about one mile east and just north of Logan. As Clark was passing through, the Gallatin Valley was in its summer phase. The mountains of the jagged Spanish Peaks, the Gallatin Range and the Bridger Range were still covered with snow and wildflowers bloomed in the valley. The buffalo trail they followed took them back and forth across several forks of the Gallatin River and by Manhattan and Belgrade as well as the future site of Bozeman. Camp on July 14th was near the mouth of Kelly Canyon about 3–4 miles east of Bozeman. The Interstate Highway approximates their route through the Gallatin Valley, up over Bozeman Pass and on down the Yellowstone River well into Eastern Montana.

 Entries for Clark on July 15th, "...*proceeded up the branch* (of the Gallatin) *to the head thence over a low gap in the mountain thence across* (most likely Jackson Creek) *passing over a low divid-ing ridge* (Bozeman Pass) *to the head of a water Course* (Billman Creek) *which runs into the Rochejhone* (Yellowstone River), *prosueing an old buffalow road keeping on the North Side of the branch to the River rochejhone at which place I arrived at 2 P M."*

Clark's mission was to explore the Yellowstone River, here just east of Livingston.
RICK AND SUSIE GRAETZ

The group of men, one woman and her child, arrived at the Yellowstone River at its "big bend" by today's Livingston. Looking south towards the Paradise Valley, *"The Roche* (Yellowstone) *passes out of a high rugid mountain* (Gallatin Range) *covered with Snow...The mountains* (Absaroka)...*on the East side of the river is rocky rugid and on them are great quantities of Snow."* Clark's route would now follow this river's course north and east to its termination where it empties its considerable waters into the Missouri River just across the Montana line in North Dakota.

This is now ranching country and the foothills expand towards some of Montana's most rugged mountains, the mighty Absaroka and Beartooth ranges on the south and the sharp peaks of the Crazy Mountains to their north. Nearing Billings, they could see the distant Pryor Mountains (named after Sergeant Nathaniel Pryor of the Expedition). Save for the development along I-90, from Livingston to Park City, the landscape remains much as it was when Clark and his followers first passed through. The river continues to flow powerful, proud, wild and free, unfettered by major dams.

Knowing they would eventually have to travel by water, the party followed the river closely and began looking for trees of ample size to make canoes. Their camp for the night of July 15th was about 3 miles below the mouth of the Shields River (named after John Shields of their party) along the Yellowstone.

Camp on July 16th was close to Big Timber in the area where the West Fork of Spring Creek meets the Yellowstone and just below Little Timber Creek. No suitable material for canoes was found on this day. At this point the Yellowstone River was gradually changing from a mountain flow to a prairie river. The water was getting warmer and the flat lands along the banks wider.

On July 17th, they encountered two major rivers entering the Yellowstone. Being opposite from each other, Clark called them the *"South and North Rivers Across."* The surge coming from the south was the present Boulder River, headwatering in the Absarokas; from the north, Big Timber Creek was meandering its way from the Crazy Mountains. Once again, no large trees were discovered, and camp that night was about two miles west of Reedpoint.

As the landscape was taking on more of a prairie look, Clark made note on July 18th that *"the hills are not exceeding 200 feet in hight ...The Country back from the river on each Side is generally open unwavering plains."* What he described is much the same as a traveler passing through the valley between Reedpoint and Billings would observe today. Noticing Indian smoke signals to the southeast, they camped just west of Columbus on a small island.

The morning of the 19th, unable these past few days to locate appropriate timber for the boats, Clark fretted, *"time is pracious as it is our wish to get to the U States this Season."* Saddling up, the party *"passed Rose bud river* (the Indian's name for today's Stillwater River)...*proceeded on about 9 miles...passed over two high points of land"* before sighting a cottonwood grove with trees large enough from which to make canoes. Halting here on the north side of the river about 2 miles south of Park City, they settled in and dubbed the place "Canoe Camp."

A survey of the area for bigger prospects proved futile, and so on the 20th, with time winding down, Clark was *"deturmined to have two Canoes made out of the largest of those trees and lash them together which will Cause them to be Study and fully Sufficient to take my Small party & Self with what little baggage we have down this river...those trees appeared tolerably Sound and will make Canoes of 28 feet in length and about 16 or 18 inches deep and from 16 to 24 inches wide."*

112

Clark noted the
landmark bluffs or
rimrocks of Billings.
LARRY MAYER

This signature at
Pompey's Pillar is the
only physical evidence
left of the Corps'
presence in Montana.
LARRY MAYER

Pompey's Pillar named
for Sacajawea's son Jean
Baptiste, or Pomp as the
men called him.
LARRY MAYER

Clark's Canoe Camp
on the Yellowstone,
July 19–24, 1806,
was near here close to
the present-day Park
City.
LAYER MAYER

Confluence of the
Bighorn and
Yellowstone rivers.
LAYER MAYER

Finding 24 of the horses missing the morning of the 21st, the search parties sent to locate them were, to quote Clark, *"unsuckcessfull."* Concerned that *"the indians (probably Crow) have Stolen our horses...I determined to have the ballance of the horses guarded"* The good news of the day was that *"the men work very diligiently on the Canoes one of them nearly finished ready to put in the water."*

The entire day of the 22nd was enthusiastically spent working on the canoes and attempting to track the horses.

Due to a tremendous work ethic and the pressures at hand, on the 23rd, *"the men finished both Canoes by 12 oClock today and I sent them to make Oars & get poles."* That afternoon, Clark *"gave Sergt Pryor his instructions...and directed that he G. Shannon & Windser take the remaining horses to the Mandans* (near Bismarck and where the Corps spent the winter of 1804–1805)...*and deliver Mr. Heney the letter* (a proposed trade arrangement to expand the American trading realm the captains had discussed with Heney, while at the Mandan villages)...*Sergt. Pryor is directed to leave the ballance of the horses with the grand Chief of the Mandans untill our arival at his village."* That evening, Clark *"had the two Canoes put into the water and lashed together ores and everything fixed ready to Set out early in the morning, at which time I have derected Sergt. Pryor to Set out with the horses and proceed on to the enterance of the big horn river* (actually today's Clark's Fork of the Yellowstone) *which we suppose to be at no great distance at which place the Canoes will meat him and Set him across the Rochejhone below the enterance of that river."*

The topography that surrounded the group at this "canoe factory" is a wonderful mix of natural features and represents the changing landscape. When Clark met the Yellowstone, he was amidst some of the state's highest peaks. As his party proceeded down the valley, the tall summits gave way to somewhat lesser forested mountains. In the vicinity of the Canoe Camp, the pine covered hills were intermingled with tall sandstone bluffs that guarded the river. As they passed beyond Billings, with the exception of distant isolated mountain groups, the terrain became more subdued and badland features were more common. The river slowed down and carried a bigger load of silt; the Yellowstone had now matured into a true prairie river and Clark's Journal writings made this clear. Today's adventurer following in the Expedition's footsteps could surely describe this interesting stretch of geography much like Clark did.

Leaving early in the morning on July 24th, passing the future sites of Laurel and Billings, Clark made note of the yellow bluffs or rimrocks as as well as the snow clad Absaroka-Beartooth Mountains and the *"Clarks fork* (Clarks Fork Yellowstone River)." On an island, east of Laurel, Clark encountered *"a large council lodge...or The lodge where all danc* (most likely a Crow Sun Dance Lodge)." A mile or so below the mouth of *"Horse* (Blue) *Creek,"* Clark helped Sergeant Pryor swim the horses across the Yellowstone, allowed Private Hall, who couldn't swim and volunteered to join and aid horsemen, to do so and bid them all a safe journey to the Mandan villages.

From this point to Glendive, I-94 follows the Yellowstone, then it's Hwy 16 to Sidney and Hwy 200 to Fairview.

Ending his first day back on the water since Three Forks, he notes *"for me to mention or give an estimate of the different Spcies of wild animals on this river particulary Buffalow, Elk Antekopes & Wolves would be incredible. I shall therefore be silent on the subject further. So it is we have a great abundance of the best meat. we made 70 ms. to day."* They spend the night on the east edge of Billings just beyond the site of today's oil refinery and where Bitter Dry Creek, coming from the south, flows into the Yellowstone.

The party was passing through Crow Country. The abundance of game, trees, water and mountains in which to escape the summer heat, made this a fine homeland for the Indians. Less than a hundred years after Clark described it, the Natives would lose it to the aggressions of the white men that followed these first explorers.

Pompey's Pillar, about 30 miles east of Billings, a prominent landmark to travelers heading through the Yellowstone Valley eastward, has been preserved as a recreation area. A trail leading to the top permits visitors to experience the same view these explorers did in 1806. William Clark's signature has been preserved as he carved it on July 25, 1806. This, to quote Gary Moulton, is *"the only surviving physical evidence of the expedition along its route."*

Jean Baptiste Charbonneau, Sacajawea's son by now a toddler, was a favorite of the Corps of Discovery. The captains affectionately called him "Pomp" or "Little Pomp". Clark named the tower as well as a stream coming into the Yellowstone directly across from this massive rock outcropping for the boy.

Clark's Journal for that day included *"at 4 P M arived at a remarkable rock Situated in an extensive bottom on the Stard. Side…this rock I ascended and from it's top had a most extensive view in every direction. This rock which I shall Call Pompy's Tower is 200 feet high and 400 paces in secumphrance and only axcessable on one Side which is from the N. E the other parts of it being a perpendicular Clift…The Indians have made 2 piles of Stone on the top of this Tower. The nativs have ingraved on the face of this rock the figures of animals &c. near which I marked my name and the day of the month & year."*

From the top of Pompey's Pillar, Clark described seeing the Bull Mountains to the northwest, the Pryor and Bighorn mountains on the southern horizon and the Wolf Mountains in a southeasterly direction. Some maps call the northern end of the Wolf Mountains the Rosebud Mountains. Almost all of the captain's southern view, encompassed today's Crow Indian Reservation.

"on the Northerly Side of the river high romantic Clifts approach &jut over the water for Some distance…back from the river for Some distance on that Side the hills are ruged & some pine back the plains are open and extensive. After Satisfying my Self Sufficiently in this delightfull prospect of the extensive Country around…I decended and proceeded on a fiew miles." They camped about four miles below Fly Creek (*"Shannons river,"* for one of his men).

On July 26th, Clark *"arrived at the enterance of Bighorn River,"* where he made his camp. He noted the *"Sof mud mixed with the Sand,"* the sand having been washed down from the deep canyons of the Bighorn about 75 miles up river. Today's Yellowtail Dam has halted much of this sand deposition, but the mud is still prevalent.

Moving on, Clark lamented, *"when we pass the Big horn I take my leave of the view of the tremendious chain of Rocky Mountain white with snow."* Encampment on July 27th was about eight miles west of Forsyth. Over time, the river has shifted to the south and this former campsite is now high and dry.

Clark was by now getting the hang of the little catamaran. The morning of the 28th, as they

▶▶ The Tongue and Yellowstone rivers mix their waters at Miles City.
LARRY MAYER

"proceeded on glideing down this Smooth Stream passing maney IsId. and Several Creeks and brooks...lower I arived at the enterance of a river...it's water like those of all other Streams which I have passed in the Canoes are muddy. I take this river to be the one the Indians Call the Little Big Horn river." This is actually Rosebud Creek, which reaches the Yellowstone at Rosebud. The current Little Bighorn River does not enter the Yellowstone, but rather meets the Bighorn River well south of the Yellowstone and near Hardin.

Clark's camp that night was just east of Hathaway across from Graveyard Creek. Though the coal the explorers passed along the banks *"is like that of the Missouri of an inferior quality,"* they were very near some of Montana's richest coal deposits. The town of Forsyth here is about 50 miles north of Colstrip an area of extensive strip mining of coal.

A headwind makes travel slow on July 29, 1806, as they pass seven *"large dry Brooks...great quantities of Coal in all the hills...late in the evening I arived at the enterance of a River which I take to be the 'Lazeka' or Tongue River...I intended to encamp on an eligable Spot imediately below this river, but finding that its' water So muddy and worm and to render it very disagreeable to drink, I crossed the rochejhone and encamped on an island close to the Lard. Shore...*on the northeastern edge of what would become Miles City, the "capital" of the big ranching country of southeastern Montana.

July 30th, *"This is by far the worst place which I have Seen on this river from the Rocky Mountains to this place a distance of,"* is how Clark described the Buffalo Sholes. They had to lower the

Cliffs of the
Yellowstone
River breaks
south of Sidney.
RICK AND SUSIE GRAETZ

canoes over them by hand for fear of breaking the boats up on the rocks. *"here is the first appearance of Birnt hills (clinker or scoria) which I have seen on this river."* Taking shelter from a violent storm, Clark noticed a nearly dry river *"and in this there is not more water than could pass through an inch auger hole. I call it Yorks dry R. (for his servant York, today's Custer Creek)...proceeded on at 7 Miles passed the enterance of a river the water...is Shallow and the water very muddy and of the Colour of the banks a darkish brown. I observe great quantities of red Stone (clinker or scoria) thrown out of this river that from the appearance of the hills at a distance on its lower Side induced me to call this red Stone (Powder) river. as the water was disagreeably muddy I could not Camp on that Side below its mouth...Crossed the river and"* camped about one half mile beyond Terry.

July 31st, *"the river approaches the high mountanious Country on the N W. Side. (Little and Big Sheep mountains) those hills appear to be composed of various Coloured earth and Coal without much rock I observe Several Conical pounds (mounds)...which appear to have been burnt (clinker or scoria) this high Country is washed into Curious formed mounds & hills and is cut much with reveens."* Clark was noting the sandstone cap rocks, formations that have a more erosion resistant rock on top of weaker material, as well as other badland topography common to southeast Montana. Camp was about eight miles southwest of Glendive across from the mouth of Whoopup Creek.

On August 1st, headwinds and rough water caused delays, they also *"Had Showers of rain repeatedly all day...My situation a very disagreeable one. In an open Canoe wet and without a possibility of keeping my Self dry...more Sand bars today than usual and more Soft mud...at 2 P. M. I was obliged to land to let the Buffalow Cross over...this gangue of Buffalow was entirely across and as thick as they could swim...I was obliged to lay to for an hour."* This day, the river travelers passed Makoshika State Park, at Glendive, a beautiful region of badlands they were unable to see because of the weather. The crew camped on an island just below the mouth of Cottonwood Creek near where Dry Creek comes into the Yellowstone. That night, *"two gangues of Buffalow Crossed a little below us, as noumerous as the first."*

Slowing down and spreading out, the *"river wide and very much divided by islands and Sand and Mud bars. the bottoms more extencive and contain more timber Such as Cotton wood ash willow...Saw emence numbers of Elk Buffalow and wolves to day...passed the enterance of Several brooks on each Side, a Small river...on the Stard. Side, which I call Ibex River (probably Smith Creek near Savage) the river in this days decent is less rapid...this morning (August 2nd) a Bear of the large vicious Species being on a Sand bar raised himself up on his hind feet and looked at us as we passed down near the middle of the river. he plunged into the water and Swam towards us, either from a disposition to attack't or from the Cent of the meat which was in the Canoes."*

Some of the islands Clark was describing are now the recreation areas of Elk Island by Savage and the Seven Sisters near Crane. This piece of the river is still very much crowded with an islands and sandbars. Canoeing from Intake to Sidney again shows nearly the same scenery Clark and his party witnessed. Experiencing this part of the Lewis and Clark Trail by river is the best way to go as the highway from Glendive to Sidney seldom nears the water to present a good view or feel for it.

In the morning of August 2nd, after passing by the future town of Sidney, Clark and his detachments paddled out of Montana for good about three miles south of Fairview. They spent the night east of Fairview on the Yellowstone River in North Dakota at the mouth of Charbonneau Creek.

After battling bears, *"buffalow gangues"* and *"musquetors,"* the scrappy crew had enough left in them to make about 86 miles on the river, one of their greatest totals of the entire journey. There are those who would say it was more like 60 miles, but hey, rivers change, we'll give it to them.

On August 3, 1806, Life was not good, *"last night the Musquetors was so troublesome that no one of the party Slept half the night. For my part I did not Sleep one hour. Those tormenting insects found their way into My beare and tormented me the whole night. They are not less noumerous or troublesome this morning. At 8. A. M. I arrived at the Junction of the Rocheejhone with the Missouri, and formed my Camp immediately...at which place the party had all encamped the 26th of April—1805...had the Canoes unloaded and every article exposed to dry & Sun."* Leaving a note for his partner, Captain Clark and his people fled down the Missouri in search of respite from the incessant *"musquetors."* After all they had endured, a tiny insect did them in.

Lewis reached the meeting of the big waters at 4pm on August 7th. Considering all the distance covered in just over one month's time (Lewis traveled an estimated 800 miles and Clark 1,000), only four days lapsed between Clark's arrival at this junction and Lewis's...well done!

On the same day, Clark managed to find a camp downriver with *"not a misquetor to be seen, which is a joyful circumstance to the Party."* The next morning, Sargeant Pryor and company arrived in camp in two round boats covered with buffalo skins. It seems as if on their second day out, all of the horses were stolen. Remembering a technique from the winter spent with the Mandans, they hurriedly built bullboats. Putting in at Pompey's Pillar, *"He informed me that they passed through the worst parts of the rapids...without taking a drop of water."* Floating along like giant teacups, they lagged several days behind Clark.

Finally, on Thursday, August 12, 1806, *"at Meridian (noon) Capt Lewis hove in Sight with the party which went by way of the Missouri as well as that which accompanied him from Travellers rest on Clarks river."* How jubilant the men must have been, to find the company whole again.

The Corps of Discovery, led by their Captains Meriwether Lewis and William Clark, arrived at St. Louis, Missouri on September 23, 1806. Their incredible Voyage of Discovery took two years, four months and nine days and they had traveled nearly 8,000 miles. In celebration Clark penned, *"descended to the Mississippi and down that river to St. Louis at which place we arrived about 12 oClock. We Suffered the party to fire off their pieces as a Salute to the Town."*